LIVING
WITH
DYING

LIVING WITH DYING

*A Guide for
Relatives & Friends*

Revised and Expanded Edition

WITHDRAWI

Glen W. Davidson

Augsburg ■ Minneapolis

LIVING WITH DYING
A Guide for Relatives & Friends

Scripture quotations unless otherwise noted are from the Revised Standard Version of the Bible, copyright © 1946, 1952, and 1971 by the Division of Christian Education of the National Council of Churches.

Cover design: Terry Dugan

Library of Congress Cataloging-in-Publication Data

Davidson, Glen W.
    Living with dying / Glen W. Davidson. — Rev. ed.
        p.   cm.
    ISBN 0-8066-2445-0
    1. Death—Psychological aspects.   2. Terminally ill—Psychology.   3. Critically ill—Psychology.   I. Title.
    BF789.D4D34   1990
    155.9'37—dc20   89-15126
                                                              CIP

The paper used in this publication meets the minimum requirements of American National Standard for Information Sciences—Permanence of Paper for Printed Library Materials, ANSI Z329.48-1984.   ∞™

Manufactured in the U.S.A.   AF-2445

94   93   92   91   90   1   2   3   4   5   6   7   8   9   10

In memory of the patients
who taught me
the meaning of
ars moriendi,
the art of dying well

Contents

A Letter to the Reader

> For everything there is a season,
> and a time for every matter under heaven:
> A time to be born, and a time to die.
> *Ecclesiastes 3:1*

This book is about dying. It is also about living. It is based on my research from interviews with more than 600 critically and terminally ill patients, their families and friends, and the health care personnel who served them. I have written the book for relatives and friends of seriously ill patients to help them better understand the emotional needs of their loved ones as well as to respect their own feelings.

"What should I do?" "What is expected of me?" "Should I be feeling this way?" These questions, and others, are among the queries relatives and friends have when someone dear to them is in health crisis.

Answers given in the book are tentative, though based on empirical data. I assume that each of us has opinions about how best to help patients cope with dying. Yet, it is the patients themselves who finally must judge which answers are appropriate to questions generated by their crises. The answers given here are tentative, not only because there is still so much to learn, but because all patients have their own ways of handling crisis. Each patient exhibits any number of ambiguities, contradictions, and inconsistencies in coping with illness. It is difficult to say anything definitive without being confronted with contradictory data.

My efforts here are directed toward understanding the ways patients try to resolve the conflict of their crises; therefore, my emphasis is on process. If you relate to someone who is critically or terminally ill, you become part of that process in living with dying. How you relate to that patient will make a difference in the ability to cope both for the patient and for yourself.

In 1960 I began delving into the ways human beings face mortality as I prepared for a dissertation entitled *Basic Images of Death in America: An Historical Analysis.* I have learned much since that first attempt to interpret my findings. The dissertation was based on works of historians, professionals in religion, and cultural analysts, but not those who were experiencing dying firsthand. Nevertheless, I gained an abiding sense of how misleading generalizations and stereotypes can be about human behavior. Stereotypes, when used literally, convey notions of fixed behavior which are not confirmed by clinical evidence. But stereotypes can also be used as figurative descriptions which permit working distinctions and identifying unique beliefs and behavior. Since each person has a unique history of experience, I intend to use stereotypes only in the latter sense. When I write that a majority of patients seemed to behave in some way or had a certain need, I hope you will take my statement as a guide by which you can better understand your loved one's uniqueness.

The origins of this book began in an internship at King's County Hospital, Brooklyn, N.Y. When my colleague, the late Carl Nighswonger, became director of the "Program on Death and Dying" at the University of Chicago Hospitals and Clinics in 1969, I began correlating clinical data gathered there with cultural and sociological data. My research continued in a fellowship at the University of Iowa Hospitals, and since 1972 at Memorial Medical Center and St. John's Hospital, two community hospitals in Springfield, Ill., that are affiliated with Southern Illinois University School of Medicine.

Since the book was first issued in 1975, I have been able to meet many more patients and colleagues who have challenged me to rethink some of my earlier assumptions. Research in thanatology has become far more sophisticated and recommendations more mature. Yet, like the earlier edition, this revision reflects my opinion that clinical data must be interpreted within the patient's context. A patient's needs in a major university teaching hospital may be different from the needs of a patient in a small community care center. What is appropriate for helping someone from one culture may not be appropriate for a patient who has been reared in another culture. The principle is that the patient needs to determine what is appropriate. Both relatives and health care staff must permit patients' feelings and needs to take priority over their own.

Living with Dying is my attempt to help relatives, friends, health care personnel, and clergy understand the patient's perspectives of living and dying so they can provide better care for patients. A companion volume, *Understanding Mourning*, focuses on how we can better care for ourselves.

The revision of *Living with Dying* was made possible by the support of my colleagues in the Department of Medical Humanities, especially Linda Keldermans who reviewed the manuscript, and Carol Faingold, Beverly Bradley, and Judie Riech who typed it. Shirlee Proctor Davidson, B.S.N., knows not only what is included, but much other data that could not be part of a short book. Together we have "lived with dying" many times, and her continuous encouragement has given me the support I needed to compose these pages.

Fictitious names are used in the examples throughout the book, but all are illustrations of authentic clinical data.

GLEN W. DAVIDSON

1

What Does Dying Mean?

You will not die. For God knows that when
you eat of it, your eyes will be opened, and you
will be like God, knowing good and evil.
Genesis 3:4-5

Dictionaries define *dying* as: "to stop living,"
"to become dead." For Bill Taylor, dying had
been as remote as a dictionary definition. It
had, that is, until his physician told him just
how serious his health crisis was. Then he had
to struggle with what dying meant for him.

Dying is given any number of definitions,
depending on cultural, religious, and historical
context. Definitions are useful to help clarify
our understandings of life's phenomena. But
understanding a phenomenon is not the same
as grasping its meaning. We can *understand*
something without any emotional involvement. But *meaning* connotes emotional involvement, and no definition is real until it is
tested in our experiences of living.

When circumstances force us to reflect on what dying means, we discover that our definition depends on what we expect from life. Our expectations shape our beliefs and values. What we expect life to be and the meaning we attach to the ending of that life define what dying means. Even if we have a fairly clear idea of what life means, most of us react with disbelief, as did Bill, when we are surprised by a health crisis.

Bill was a 50-year-old truck driver fighting a serious lung disease. "When I came in here, I believed that I would never really die; I thought death is only an illusion," he said. "When I was told what I have, when I realized that I would die because of it, I felt like I had been hit by a Mack truck! I couldn't believe it. I couldn't talk about it. I wanted to, but I just couldn't find the right words. I didn't even know the right questions to ask. I guess I've lived as though things would always be the same."

Bill's expectations for living were, in one sense, uniquely his own. Out of his expectations, he developed a fairly elaborate ethic about what is appropriate and what is offensive in his life. Initially, he judged his illness to be offensive and his suffering to be inappropriate. That meant that either he or someone else was at fault. In another sense, his expectations reflected the cultural, religious, sociological, and psychological contexts in which he lived.

At first, Bill was too startled by his health crisis to be very reflective about his expectations. Later, he became aware of and confused by the contradiction between his expectations for unending life and the realities of his illness. At first he couldn't function with the ordinary decisions of life; then the contradiction, not the illness, startled him. As he worked through the contradiction in his mind, he began to adjust to living with illness, and life, for him, took on new meaning.

Like Bill, you may never have given much thought to your expectations for life. Dying, for you, may have been as remote as a dictionary definition—until a health crisis startled you into reflecting about what life really means to you. If so, it is important to understand that your expectations for life do not need to be consistent, rational, or orderly. Few people are so rigid as to hold themselves to consistent expectations. The point is not whether you are consistent or inconsistent in your expectations, but whether you can overcome being dysfunctional if you discover that you hold unrealistic expectations for life.

Bill's health crisis rudely awakened him to the unrealistic expectations he had for life and he felt betrayed. His awareness was the occasion of great suffering. As he struggled to make sense of his suffering, his expectations for life changed. Finally, the occasion of Bill's suffering became the experience through which he resolved his conflict and he began again to function in the routines of living. Following Bill through his health crises is to follow a process by which he attempted to resolve conflicts of meaning:

If I expect life to be unending,
then dying seems to be an illusion.

When Bill's life was fairly secure and routine, it was easy for him to assume that life, his at least, would continue uninterrupted. He saw tragedy striking others, but with care and determination he thought he could preserve his own.

Bill believed staunchly that he would never die—not the "real Bill." When he began to receive visitors at the hospital, he kept assuring them he would be "just fine in no time" even though he knew his diagnosis. When his physical appearance began to deteriorate, he would ask rhetorically, "Don't we believe in immortality?" For Bill, personal immortality was the basic tenet of his faith. He believed himself to be naturally immortal.

When his friends from church came to visit, they spoke about how he must maintain "Christian hope." With this statement, they seemed to mean that if Bill would keep up his will and his hopes remained high, he could overcome his disease and leave the hospital as good as new. Dying was an illusion to them, too.

Holding to this interpretation of life carries at least two risks. The first is that such a faith does not permit the person experiencing crisis to acknowledge basic change and real loss. When Bill's health began to deteriorate markedly, he began to question whether he had real faith. His friends tried to encourage him with declarations that if he kept up his faith, he would be as good as new. By implication, this inference suggested to Bill that if he did not recover, it would be because his faith had not been strong enough. When Bill did not become as good as new, these friends ceased coming to see him.

The second risk of this interpretation is that it depends on an outdated understanding of biology. In the days when we knew very little about the mind, it was assumed that the mind was a separable entity from the body because it was thought to be the seat of the soul. In those days, there was no awareness of how hormones and blood circulation can alter basic thought patterns as well as behavior patterns. "Train the mind properly," "believe correctly," "have the right kind of faith," and nothing that happened to the body could touch the mind.

We now know that our minds and the thoughts we have are integral to and largely dependent on a relatively healthy body. As a matter of discipline for living a healthy and moral life, we do need to train our minds. Mind training, though, does not prevent us from living with consequences of bodily failure or from struggling with the suffering produced when our expectations do not conform to reality. Nor are we released from the guilt we feel when we are not able to will away our dying.

If I live life as a vocation,
then dying is an intrusion.

Bill began to shift interpretation of his health crisis from dying as an illusion to dying as an intrusion. Had he not been living a good, moral life? Had he not been one of the best drivers on the road? When his buddies from work came to see him, they reminisced about Bill's adventures and exploits: how he was the one to drive through the worst storm of the year; how he had been shot at when defying a wildcat strike; how he never had a road accident. "What a great guy you are, Bill! What a shame this is happening to you."

Bill did find some comfort in reflecting on the good he had done in his life. "Dying may be cutting off my life, but it can't take away from me what I've done." For Bill, this interpretation was but a transition. There are many of us, however, who use similar interpretations of life as our religion. "Life is defined by the good we do." Hope is based on the expectation that one can live long enough and well enough to complete one's purpose in living life as a mission, and most of us get considerable satisfaction from our vocation, as long as we can see the good we do. Let the times change, however, let our vocation no longer be needed, let a new generation choose different styles of living, let us be forgotten, and we risk losing our sense of worth. Then the "real I" is not only intruded upon by dying but consumed by feelings of worthlessness.

If life is a threat,
then dying is an escape.

Bill's disease became very painful. Medications relieved his pain for a time, but they also dulled his mind. Bill wanted to be able to converse with his family, so he resisted taking any more medication than necessary. As each breath became more and more painful, as he saw the suffering of his family, life became a threat. Bill found himself wondering if the joys and happiness of life had all been an illusion. He prayed to die so that he could escape both the pain of his disease and the suffering of his conflicts.

Interpretation of life as a threat was a new experience for Bill. He had always felt quite secure. Some people, however, know life only as oppression and insecurity. Few moments are free from wondering where the next threat to survival will come. Religion for them becomes a matter of survival through escape. For them, hope is based on the expectation that they will be able to attain a place or a status free from the forces that seem to be destroying them.

Whatever the reasons for this interpretation of life—whether social, family, or personal crisis—death as an escape carries a risk. While release from pain and terror may be desired, it may be so overwhelming a concern that our conflicts, such as those of love and loss, are ignored. This interpretation is so self-centered it does not permit release from interpersonal conflict between sufferers and those touched by their suffering. Like medication that only dulls the senses, the meaning of death as an escape releases the sufferer from pain but not from the cause of the suffering. But then, sometimes, a person is given no other option.

If I accept life as a gift,
then dying is part of the given.

Before the advent of modern hospital care, dying patients could complete one final task— to teach their relatives and friends how to "die well." In the Middle Ages, preparation to die was called *ars moriendi*—the art of dying well. Little books of devotions were written, not to picture the ravages of the plague or to warn the reader of the consequences for failing to prepare for one's end, but to give "a complete and intelligible guide to the business of dying, a method to be learned while one is in good health and kept at one's fingers' ends for use in that all-important and inescapable hour."[1] While well, Bill would have resisted looking at such a book. His conscious efforts had been directed to the belief that life was unending. Ironically, the fairly slow progress of his disease, with as much suffering as it caused, permitted Bill to work through his interpretation of living to the point that he could affirm life, yet accept his own dying.

When he tried to pretend that he did not really have a disease, that dying was an illusion, Bill had hoped for the miracle that would turn the clock back to the time when life was routine and he felt secure. To give the weight of sacred authority to his expectation, he proclaimed his wish as "Christian hope." When he no longer could manage the pretense of health, he based his hopes for worth on his vocation and the good works he had performed. After several months of illness, not only his good works, but he, himself, seemed to have been forgotten. His close friends seemed to have tired of coming to visit. And his interpretation of dying as an escape spoke more to the pain of living than his sense of self-worth.

When Bill began to reflect on how precious, though fragile, life is, on how quickly security can become insecurity, on how basic change seems to characterize life, he learned to interpret his life in an entirely different way. Confessionally, gently, he spoke of how so much of what he treasured in life had come not as a reward because he deserved it or because he had earned it, but as a gift. Maybe dying was a part of that gift. Maybe he had overlooked the real meaning of his life. Rather than being obsessed with preserving himself, he began to reach out to his family to share the suffering they had in common. Ironically, as he adjusted to the realities of his crisis, as he permitted himself to let go of old expectations, as he touched and allowed himself to be touched with love, he was released from his conflict. He still was in pain and he continued to degenerate physically, but now he could affirm life and face his dying.

This interpretation of life carries a profound risk with it, too. It requires acknowledging loss, pain, suffering, frustrated desires, and uncompleted goals as parts of living. Rather than affirming human perfectibility, it acknowledges personal frailty. The idea is based on the premise that even though human beings are mortal, mortal characteristics do not cut one off from the purpose of life. To put this in theological language: neither loss, nor suffering, nor even dying, can cut us off from the Giver of life.

The art of dying has not been lost, though for most of us the scene and setting for its dramatic resolution have shifted from the intimacy of the home to the public life of the hospital. What Bill discovered during his hospitalization was that he could "die well" but not, as he put it, "until I found out that it was the devil who sold me that bill of goods about never dying."

Whether you have identified with any of Bill's interpretations of life is not as important as understanding that the meaning of dying is based on our expectations for living. When crisis comes, we will discover that as our expectations for living change, so too will the meaning of dying. "For where your treasure is, there will your heart be also" (Matt. 6:21).

CAN WE ALLOW DYING TO BE PART OF LIFE?

Whether we allow dying to be part of our lives has profound consequences. Bill's transition in understanding what dying meant for him is not unusual for critically and terminally ill patients whose health crises give them time to work through their interpretations of the experience. Many of the hundreds of patients I have followed experienced a similar release. But some patients never were released from the suffering of their conflicts. Some of them weren't given the time. Others were not to be released because of demands and expectations imposed on them by well-meaning relatives, friends, or health care workers whose own feelings became primary.

While a loved one's health crisis is always a shock, if we cannot accept the realities of the health crisis or adapt as fast as patients do, we tend to act defensively in an apparent effort to protect our own emotions. This is called the "abandonment syndrome." Almost all patients express fear that their condition will make them so unacceptable to those around them that they will be abandoned. Numerous studies have confirmed their fears. Patients admitted to a health care center are faced with a double burden: wrestling with survival and struggling to learn new expectations of those on whom they rely for their needs. The familiar presence of family and friends consequently becomes even more important. The patient may feel abandoned as the result of any of these occasions:

1. *A brief and formal monologue.* A physician, for example, may pop in on the patient, ask a few rhetorical questions such as, "You're looking better today, aren't you?" and leave, appearing too busy to listen to intimate fears. A member of the clergy may call on a parishioner, say a few words of good cheer, offer a formalized prayer, and leave without ever knowing what is really troubling the patient. Nurses

may place dying patients in dark corners of a ward, stop at the bedside only long enough to check vital signs, or make only mandatory visits. Friends and relatives may breeze in, inform them how they ought to be feeling, promise to stop by the next day, and never return.

2. *Treating patients as though their disease or accident has turned them into nonpersons.* This kind of abandonment is evident whenever visitors or staff talk about patients in front of them as though they are not there anymore. Even unconscious patients may hear.

3. *Ignoring or rejecting patients' attempts to discuss their interpretations of what is going on.* If a woman says, "I think I'm going to die soon," and we respond, "Nonsense, you're not the only patient to feel like this, you know," we have informed her that her feelings are not important.

4. *Literal abandonment*—especially with patients in nursing homes. Many well-meaning, close friends and relatives say that they no longer visit loved ones in a hospital or nursing home because: "I want to remember him the way he was," or "She doesn't even remember my name," or "Everything that can be done is being taken care of by the nurses," or "Everyone has to die alone." Perhaps being with the

28

patient is too threatening. But even senile patients need to be physically stroked, spoken to, and given gestures of affection.

We may be so troubled by fears of death or be so shocked by the implications of a loved one's crises that we have to separate ourselves from them in some way. Abandonment is the most effective short-term defense mechanism we have, but it doesn't help the patient.

Many suggestions have been made to correct the abandonment syndrome. One suggestion often made is to "let the patient return home to die." For some patients this may be an appropriate suggestion, but not for all. We need to remember that close friends and relatives in the homes are as susceptible to the temptation to abandon patients as hospital personnel. Some patients may receive competent care at home, but many may not. The recurring statement, "I'm so thankful to be here in the hospital; now maybe I can get some peace," is a grim reminder that patients often find themselves in conflict with well-meaning relatives whose own needs are not accommodated easily to the needs of the patients.

My suggestion to correct the abandonment syndrome is to remind friends, relatives, and health care personnel that patients need all of them because together they tend to balance one another's talents and deficiencies. Hospital personnel have skills that few relatives, even those trained as nurses or doctors, can provide. Part of their expertise is made possible by an emotional distance that allows them to accept patient needs for what they are. These needs may be too threatening to grieving friends and relatives. Yet, try as they may, hospital personnel cannot give the kind of personal affection a patient has come to trust from family and friends. Each relative and friend is a unique individual. Each can respond to the patient in a special way. Each can bring a different emotional strength that may help the patient regain a sense of equilibrium.

All of us—relatives, friends, or health care personnel—tend to abandon patients when something about their crises threatens our own emotional stability. No one can pretend to meet all of a patient's needs. Only as we recognize our own limitations and work together can we overcome the abandonment syndrome. Only as we work through those things that threaten us emotionally can we adequately respect our own health.

What does dying mean? When it is not a part of the phenomena of our life or that of a loved one, it may have no apparent meaning. When dying touches us or one of our loved ones, it may be so threatening that we must deny it is part of life. But whatever it means, it is based on the expectations we have of life. For some of us, dying means the experience of discovering who we really are. Then dying becomes the most revelatory event of our lives.

2

When Dying Means Loss

Blessed are those who mourn,
for they shall be comforted.
Matthew 5:4

Dying may be defined in many ways, but universal to all definitions is loss—separation from persons we love, from places or objects we treasure, from a part of our self-identity. We develop an understanding of dying from the way we have learned to cope emotionally with the wounds of loss.

When we, or those close to us, are dying, we *feel* the loss. Some of us are very guarded about showing our emotions. We have not learned adequately what to do with our feelings. Those of us who have learned to be more open and honest with our feelings have the best prognosis for healing from loss.

John was a muscular 48-year-old assembly line worker. The death of his mother was a devastating blow. Though John took great pride in his strength and to his friends appeared emotionally strong, he was quite dependent on his mother and relied on her even after his marriage. He seemed to have exaggerated feelings of competition about his work and his play. He always had to win. Consequently, he never permitted himself to appear as losing. Even though his mother had been dead six months, he would not mention her name or allow others to do so in his presence. It seemed at first as though he felt no loss, but after a time he became sullen, depressed, and aloof.

Mike also worked on an assembly line. He lost his parents in an automobile accident when he was 42 years old. Initial reaction to the death of his parents was shock, but then he cried freely, talked about his childhood experiences with his family, and participated in overt rituals of mourning with his wife and children. Mike had always been a warm, friendly person, but of more importance emotionally, he did not feel he always had to win. He could tell jokes on himself and he readily acknowledged mistakes.

LEARNING TO COPE WITH LOSS

We are born with the *ability* to adapt to change, but we all must *learn* how to cope with loss.

If you are able to read this book, you have already learned some rituals for coping with your losses. Not all ways for coping are healthy ways, however. I think it is no accident that the reason I came to know John and Mike is that John was admitted to the hospital with cancer of the colon 11 months after his mother's death. I met Mike when he came to visit John. Clinical studies show that despite obvious differences in family composition, religion, ethnic origin, and socioeconomic status, repressing feelings over loss prevents us from adapting to the change loss has thrust into our lives and may lead to mental and physical breakdown.

What do we need to learn in order to cope with loss? First, we need to learn to respect the natural psychological process that helps us recover emotionally from the shock of loss and from the suffering of deprivation. Our natural way is to mourn or grieve. To mourn is to ventilate feelings. This ventilation sets us to working through emotions and expectations associated with what we are losing or have lost. Mourning involves testing the reality of permanent absence, reassessing identification with the loved person, reexamining our expectations of the loved person, and transferring to and investing emotionally in new people.

Not all of us have learned to mourn effectively. How the following children were taught
may make the point clear. Pat, a single parent,
thought that each of her children should have
a pet. "It builds responsibility," she said. She
daily monitored the children's feeding, clean-
ing, and caring of the pets, but she never did
their chores for them. One day she noticed
that her daughter's goldfish was floating up-
side down. Quick scrutiny revealed that the
fish was already dead. When her daughter
came home, Pat allowed her to discover her
loss. Together, they took the fish out of the
bowl and put it in fresh water. Within reason,
Pat cooperated with every other suggestion
her daughter made for trying to revive the pet.
Finally, the little girl cried, "My fish is dead,"
and Pat could comfort her. Not until that point
would the little girl tolerate being comforted.
Pat helped her daughter make a cardboard cof-
fin and together they buried the cherished pet
in the back yard. No suggestion was made
about replacing the fish until it came from the
little girl. Until then Pat helped her daughter
grieve over the lost goldfish. Pat used rituals
of openness and acceptance to instruct her children. The day came when the little girl an-
nounced that she was ready for a new pet. She
had been healed.

Gloria instructed her children differently—with rituals of denial and defensiveness. She objected to her son, Pete, having a dog. She doubted that he would take very good care of it. There were frequent lapses of responsibility when Gloria had to care for the pet; nevertheless, the dog seemed a healthy outlet for Pete's affections. One afternoon, the dog was hit by a car. Gloria was horrified. Frantically, she buried the remains in the back lawn and scrubbed the pavement so that the child would not see any stains when he returned from school. After checking with her husband, she dashed to the local pet store and had a new pet waiting for Pete when he came home. There was not much emotion expressed in their household, either joy or sorrow. Gloria answered Pete's questions honestly, though reluctantly. But she kept emphasizing that he had a new dog; he ought not mourn. When the boy cried, his father informed him, "Real men don't cry!"

Gloria, like many parents, did not want to inflict suffering on her children. "They will have to face up to that soon enough as it is." She tried to pretend that the new puppy would fill any place in Pete's emotions left empty by the death of his dog. While "it just seemed best" to Gloria, she had robbed her son both of the opportunity to learn that loss can be faced openly and that his feelings were appropriate. Denial is our first reaction to loss. Gloria unwittingly tried to make it the lasting reaction. Rather than keeping her children from knowing about irreversible loss and suffering, she conveyed to them the notion that loss, and their emotions as a reaction to loss, are taboo.

Both mothers were well-meaning. Pat respected her daughter's feelings and as a result helped the girl learn to honor the natural way of healing. Because Gloria and her husband were uncomfortable with their own emotions, Pete's expression of grief was threatening to them. Their behavior taught Pete that he ought not trust his own feelings. Healing from his loss would be difficult.

If the first thing we need to learn in order to cope with loss is to respect our emotions of mourning, the second is to learn that mourning is a developmental and lifelong process. We can expect to mourn only within the limits of our emotional capacity. When loss is encountered as a child, grieving primarily is a feeling. When loss is encountered as an adolescent, grieving is both a feeling and a concept. When loss is encountered as an adult, grieving is not only a feeling and a concept, but also an evaluated behavior. Following is a brief description of how we develop our capacity for mourning.

THE CHILD'S ENCOUNTER WITH LOSS

The way children react to loss depends largely on their emotional age.[2] Children feel pain and they suffer emotionally, but they do not have adult logic by which to understand the experience. Consequently, their mourning is often abbreviated and left incomplete.

Infants who lose their mother through death or abandonment in the second or third month seem to experience distress when the "motherfigure" is changed, but distress can be relieved as long as the infant's needs are satisfied.[3] Loss experienced between six months and one year causes more serious distress because the infant has become able to distinguish between what satisfies needs and who does the satisfying. Should loss occur, the child does not automatically transfer emotional attachment for the mother to someone else.

Loss can be quite a shock to young children because they have no innate notion that life ever ceases. Before age four, children may begin to ask questions about dying, questions stimulated by the phenomena of autumn, death of a favorite pet, or the loss of a cherished person. Their questions assume that there is a reason for everything. While they generally are not interested in the physiological aspects of death, they do want to know, "Where did Grandma go?" "Why?" "How?" They may ask the same questions over and over again. Because children do not have a well-developed conceptual framework by which to interpret the answers, their questions seem new to them even though they appear redundant to adults.

A little boy of five is able to see relationships, some causations, and some implications, but he usually is unable to put himself in another person's position. Therefore, he has great difficulty handling other people's mourning. One family received word of the death of a beloved grandmother. When his parents and two older sisters began to cry, Jimmie did, too. Then he began to laugh. Indignantly, his sisters demanded that he explain his behavior. "Well, she will be back, won't she? Why be sad?"

We all have a limited capacity for grieving, but children are even more limited. Often confused by the seemingly long rituals adults use for grieving, children are usually ready to return quickly to their routine rhythms of living.

Children's initial reaction to loss is denial. Their rhythms of mourning usually are broken by periods of denial and "make believe," either that the crisis has never happened, or that they have the magical power to make the deceased come back alive. What impact denial has on emotional development depends largely on how well adults around the children react to their behavior. A college student reported that when he returned home from school as a first-grader, he was told that his older sister had "gone away" and would never come back. Out of bewilderment, he asked questions, only to have his parents respond with evasiveness. Finally, they ordered him to stop asking questions. Through the child's thought processes, which tend to be egocentric and concrete, he assumed that he must have done something wrong and that is why his sister went away. He suffered with his unmentionable guilt until he took a course about death and dying in college.

Young children evaluate events of loss in terms of the repercussions. For the college student whose sister died when he was a first-grader, the repercussion was guilt. For another college student, it was anger. Sarah had been a "dying child." She reported that while she knew something was basically wrong, both from the way that she felt and the way people acted around her, her questions were rebuffed.

An embarrassed nurse retorted that she was a "very naughty girl" for asking her questions about dying. In her bewilderment, infected by increasing anger, Sarah had the most distorted of fantasies. Sometimes she believed she was being eaten alive by frogs. At other times she pictured the doctors and nurses as wizards and witches who were changing her into an animal. Her mother and father appeared in her dreams as miniature toys, utterly helpless. Sarah alternated between roles of a little girl screaming for their help and of a heroine trying to rescue them. What was happening to her was incomprehensible. She had intense feelings but an inability to interpret the experience. Now as an adult, she works with critically ill children and tries to help them "have a different ending to their nightmares."

Children use a great deal of fantasy in their efforts to grasp inexplicable phenomena. In the illustrations above, I have focused on children who have experienced loss firsthand. But children between the ages of five and puberty also work through notions concerning dying and loss in peer relationships. They speculate and create games. They play at "what it must be like." Anne Hebert Smith tells about a group of children in North Carolina waiting for their dance class to begin. They acted out their curiosity concerning dying by chanting:

"Well, what's the news?"
  "Well, what is the news?"
"Aunt Donna's dead!"
  "Aunt Donna's dead?"
"Well how did she die?"
  "Well how did she die?"
"Well, she died like this."
  "She died like this?"
"Ugh! Ugh! Ugh!" (acted out with mock agony)

If adults don't oppress their initiative, children's questions concerning death arise from curiosity about how change through loss could have occurred. Some children express profound confusion in fantasy and bizarre games. Recent research suggests that all children have some confusion about inevitable and irreversible loss.

Because children have feelings but an incomplete capacity for interpreting the experience that stimulates these feelings, their healing process usually is incomplete until late adolescence or adulthood. If children are encouraged to share emotions and their perceptions, they learn that they still are acceptable and lovable despite their loss. They can continue to grow emotionally as well as physically.

THE ADOLESCENT'S ENCOUNTER
WITH LOSS

Adolescents are of an age when they can understand the full implications of dying and the finality of death. They have the capacity both for feeling and interpreting experiences of loss, including well-developed ways for testing reality and for adapting to the change loss brings. Generally, however, the overt behavior of adolescents is significantly different from the patterns of mourning among mature adults. Like children, adolescents tend to overcompensate for feelings of grief by fantasizing either return of the loved person or power to reverse the loss. The intensity of this contradiction in behavior seems to be in direct proportion to adolescent progress in establishing independence from parents. The more insecure adolescents are in their own identities, the more they try to overcompensate for inadequacies.

Normal adolescents, whether having developed a very strong self-concept or a weak one within the family structure, must be able to identify those points that differentiate them from their parents before they can become autonomous adults. To achieve this distinction, they come to recognize that they no longer are dependent on adults. Thus, it is common to turn to peers for identity support. It is from close peer competitors that a boy, for example, can estimate his own prowess—whether his mind is keen, his body is strong, his accomplishments worthy. It is from her peers that a girl learns what is mature and what is immature, even though the peer group's definitions may be quite at odds with those of adults. Hair and clothing styles often reflect the definitions of the peer group. At the same time, however, adolescents need parents or other authority figures to help set limits in order to have a mark by which to measure development into adulthood.

Research on the emotional needs of adolescents in times of crisis suggests that the overwhelming majority fear loss of those closest to them—both their friends and family. They also fear isolation. Unfortunately, at the time adolescents need support from family they also seek peer approval from peers who often set themselves in opposition to an adult's identity. Competition between peers and parents to influence adolescent behavior produces conflict under very normal circumstances. This conflict becomes intense in a crisis of loss. Adolescent signals of needs may be confusing to adults, as, in fact, those feelings are confusing to adolescents themselves. Both close fellowship and solitude are important for adolescents in crisis. Every adolescent needs access to adults who are loving and tolerant of erratic behavior.

In *All Grown Up & No Place to Go*, psychologist David Elkind argues that in today's hurried society children, even the most ambitious adolescents, have difficulty finding real work for real rewards.[4] Those adolescents struggling with disease, who are not permitted by well-meaning adults to struggle with the reality of their disease in ways that seem "real" to them, are either forced back into a posture of infant dependency or into exaggerated rebellion for independence. For adolescents who are patients themselves, it is bad enough that they must wrestle with a body deteriorating at the same time that their peers are filling out in the full bloom of maturity, but it is intolerable to have a sense of worth snatched away either by those they love or with whom they compete.

While adolescents have capacities for both feeling and conceptualizing experiences of loss, their judgments about the implications of their experiences are often quite immature and their healing may be left incomplete. Often an adolescent treats all loss with the same intensity. When Bob lost his favorite coat, for example, he thought his life was ruined. Mary thought she could never recover when her boyfriend left her, but she was as emotionally distraught over losing her athletic pin. Unlike children, adolescents have the capacity to conceptualize experiences of loss. Unlike adults, however, they have not had the experience to place their losses in any kind of priority or hierarchy of values. One mark of maturity is the ability to differentiate degrees of loss in which disrupted relationships mean more than misplaced possessions.

An adolescent's encounter with loss is far less affected by whether adults respond with exactly the right words as by the "feeling tones" with which they respond. If adults convey that feelings of, or questions about, loss are inappropriate, adolescents are thwarted in their mourning. Only as they are encouraged to express themselves and to evaluate what loss means can they resolve the conflicts of their experience and thereby be free to move on to discover new concerns, curiosities, and joys of living.

THE ADULT'S ENCOUNTER WITH LOSS

By the time many of us reach adulthood, we have learned that our days are numbered, and we try to live our lives wisely. However, to know that we are mortals does not keep us from feeling the excruciating sting of loss. Hopefully our knowledge does permit us to trust that even though we experience irreversible loss, we are given the capacities to go on living. Mature mourning permits us to adapt to change forced by loss.

John Bowlby and C. Murray Parkes identify four phases of healthy mourning: (1) numbness, (2) yearning for the deceased person or lost object, (3) disorganization and despair, and (4) reorganization.[5]

Numbness is a characteristic of emotional shock and is exhibited both by outright denial that loss has taken place and by stupor. Some people may believe that they are functioning normally at a time of loss, but objective observation indicates the contrary.

The second phase is characterized by painful yearning for the deceased person or lost object. The mind becomes obsessed with everything that can be recalled about the deceased. Familiar sounds and smells may, at least momentarily, make mourners believe that their loved ones have returned. Anger at being left alone, guilt over omissions in their relationship, and separation from familiar patterns of life shared with another—all these emotions deepen the pain of separation.

The period of disorganization is marked by the struggles of survivors to compensate for the roles no longer played by the deceased. In the family constellation, there are problems over who will assume vacated roles. For a surviving spouse, there not only is the need to compensate for former dependence on the deceased but the uncertainty over what degree of independence is either possible or desirable.

Reorganization usually occurs gradually. Some people seem to be relieved of their grief in a relatively short time. In some cultures, the period of reorganization is marked by a ritual, such as a feast on the anniversary of the death, which signals that the period of mourning is over. What is important is when, in one's heart, the deceased is permitted to be released. Then healing takes place, and love may again be directed to others.

Adults who suffer loss of someone close sometimes mourn with behavior more appropriate to a child. Analysis usually uncovers unresolved loss from childhood or adolescence, evidence that for some reason the mourning process was left incomplete. Mark is an example.

Mark was 35 when his mother died. He appeared to have a stable home life and a satisfying career, but he began to exhibit erratic behavior soon after his mother's funeral. He failed to complete assignments at work, his sleep patterns were disturbed, and he seemed aloof from his family. When Mark came for therapy, he said he was coming to satisfy his family, that there was nothing wrong with him. Yet, even in the first session, he broke into tears and began to speak of "Auntie." When asked why he called his mother Auntie, he reacted with surprise. "I don't. That is what I called my aunt." Mark remembered his aunt as a surrogate mother. She had lived next door to his parents, had provided him with a great deal of companionship, and had taken care of him while his mother was confined to bed with a long illness. Auntie had died when Mark was 12. The occasion of his mother's death stimulated repressed conflict. Mark, as a child, had not been able to understand his aunt's death and in his subconscious, at least, he had tried to keep her within grasp.

Mourning is our natural way of healing from loss. When our grieving process is healthy, we are able to express our feelings, conceptualize or make sense out of the experience, and we are able to come to a weighted assessment of what the experience means to us. Not every loss will be felt with the same intensity.

OUR ENCOUNTER WITH ANOTHER'S LOSS

Even though we may have developed healthy ways for handling loss, we may fall into what I call the "surrogate suffering syndrome" when we encounter another's loss. It is one thing to work through our own feelings of loss; it is quite another to realize that we must let others work through their sense of loss, too. Most of us try to shield our loved ones from suffering, particularly when the one loved is a child. But, as noted above, even children must be able to work through feelings of loss. The following examples demonstrate why.

Two six-year-old children had leukemia. Martha, mother of the first child, had great difficulty handling her own emotions. She was often hysterical, anxious, and guilt-ridden. She conveyed to both her friends and the hospital personnel that no one should permit her child to suffer. "Don't explain anything to him. Don't play with him. Leave him to me." Her child, in turn, reflected the emotions and behavior of his mother, largely it seemed because those were the emotions she would accept from him. Each step of therapy was a hassle. Panic seemed to infect the child every time someone came into his room. He was confused and frightened.

Geri, mother of the second child, maintained a sense of composure, courage, and competence even though there were times when she cried freely. She identified times and circumstances when she needed help from others, particularly from her husband, and assumed a healthy dependence on the hospital staff. Her son exhibited similar behavior. Even as he was dying, he insisted that he do some things for himself. Despite the usual side effect of his disease and therapy, which sometimes led to disorientation and depression, the patient seemed to have a sense of confidence that he would be taken care of. For both children, the disease was debilitating. But for the first child, there was additional suffering with fears of being unable to cope.

The attempt to shoulder a person's suffering for them is as futile as it is to try to do their dying for them. The attempt seems to be motivated by a mixture of goodwill and guilt, love and hostility, service and need to control. Every attempt to be the surrogate sufferer imposes an additional burden of loss on the person dying.

Attempts to be another's surrogate sufferer and attempts to stifle personal feelings are not healthy ways to handle loss. Mourning is our natural way for coping with loss. When our grieving process is healthy, we are able to express our feelings, conceptualize or make sense out of the experience, and we are able to come to a weighted assessment of what the experience means to us. "Blessed are those who mourn, for they shall be comforted."

3

When Dying Means Change

For every matter has its time and way, although
man's trouble lies heavy upon him.

Ecclesiastes 8:6

Dying means change. Even when we think we
are prepared, as the time approaches most of
us fear we will not be able to cope. The adage,
"every matter has its time and way," is appli-
cable, though. We not only change but we can
adapt to the realities of most crises no matter
how offensive or radical.

Change may not be our true fear, however.
Many patients and relatives initially insist that
they feared they could not change. On further
reflection they discovered they were far more
threatened by the possibilities that they would
lose their humanness or their dignity in the
process of change.

Dignity ought not be confused with pride.

Pride implies an exaggerated sense of self-worth and is the opposite of humility. Both a proud and humble person have a sense of dignity. Dignity stands for the self-assessment we have of ourselves as persons. It is the sense of worth that comes with having the freedom and responsibility to make judgments about what is proper and improper. Self-reliance—the ability to make decisions for oneself—was the word most frequently used by patients to describe what dignity meant to them. It may have been the decision whether to submit to surgery or to chemotherapy. It may have been making the simple choice of whether they would eat jello or cottage cheese for lunch. But it was *their* decision. We acknowledge the dignity of others when we honor their sense of propriety and their right to make decisions about themselves.

We are changed by dying. The process of change, whether for patient or for family and friends, follows a fairly common pattern of behavior.[6] We feel shocked, then we need to ventilate our feelings of anguish. Given time, we are able to reassess who we are as a result of the changes forced on us. Perhaps we can relate better to others, and be addressed by them, with dignity if we understand the psychodynamics of change.

WHEN WE ARE IN SHOCK

Shock is the first psychodynamic in adapting to change forced on us by health crises and usually takes one of two forms: denial or panic. Denial is what has been called the human shock-absorber to tragedy. It is the way our emotions are desensitized temporarily and our sense of time temporarily suspended in an attempt to delay the consequences of the crisis. This permits us to "have time" to marshal inner resources and to search for an appropriate response to an otherwise overwhelming threat.

Judy's behavior is an example of the use of denial. Judy was a beautiful young woman. Until her automobile accident she had been vivacious and healthy. Afterward, her injuries left her paralyzed from the waist down. Any parent knows the infant's immense sense of achievement after learning to sit up, crawl, and then walk. Her loss of mobility was devastating for her. Psychologically, it took Judy much longer than it took her friends and relatives to adapt to the realities of her accident. She would greet visitors with the demand, "Nothing is wrong, so don't be upset!" Not unlike dazed accident victims in the emergency room who rise up off a stretcher despite broken bones and injured organs, Judy could not function realistically.

The appearance of shock and the use of denial may be quite inconsistent. To one person, such as the physician or the spouse, the patient may show massive denial: "I'm all right!" To another person, such as a sympathetic friend, nurse, or chaplain, the patient may be quite open with personal feelings. It may not seem appropriate to share some realizations with some people; with others the patient may share deepest feelings. Why? The patient may feel safer by holding people with professional responsibilities at a distance. Or the patient may be able to sense that those closest to them are in shock themselves. Perhaps the patient's sense of propriety has been violated. The health care staff may have been curt toward the patient. Perhaps the patient's sense of modesty was violated. Sometimes unwitting but hurtful things were said. These, and similar situations, make the patient feel loss of personal dignity. Shock results.

Denial sometimes takes the form of displaced concern. Some patients can be in critical condition, yet deny any concern for themselves while expressing great concern about others. Sometimes denial takes the form of what is meant to be objective observation. This form of denial is frequently used by relatives. They may be deeply shocked about their loved one's health crisis, yet they try to act as though they are emotionally detached. All of these forms of denial lack the spontaneity that would be an expression of true feelings—anger, terror, offendedness. In denial, feelings are temporarily frozen.

Panic is the opposite of denial. When all structures of stability in our lives seem to have been destroyed our emotions have no limit to expression. Hysteria, agitation, or self-destructive behavior are forms of panic. Whatever the form, to the person in panic, "the world has come apart." Intense anxiety, exaggerated excitement, or paranoidal ideas may occur for a short duration. Providing no physical harm results, such manifestations of panic can be brought under control by someone exercising calm and authoritative leadership. Of longer duration, these manifestations of panic may need the assistance of a psychiatrist. Frequently a person in panic will grind through all emotional gears in a desperate attempt to find one that will work to restore a sense of order. "Where can I turn, where can I turn?" was the one coherent phrase used by a woman whose denial had been stripped away. Her world had become topsy-turvy.

Several general principles may guide relatives, friends, and health care staff to help a person in shock:

1. We need to be as calm as we can and avoid inconsistency and judgmentalism. In shock, especially if bordering on panic, we need to let someone who can be more detached offer primary care. There is nothing more contagious than panic, nor more reassuring than calmness, to a person in shock.

2. We need to use calm but direct and specific language, speaking to the individual by name and with direct eye contact.

3. We may need to assist the person to become reoriented by identifying for him or her such factors of reality as time, place, and the names of familiar people.

4. We should, as much as possible, avoid trying to force the person in shock to make decisions while in shock.

5. We must respect denial mechanisms as a person copes with crisis. We all use denial from time to time as a defense mechanism in our attempts to replace the chaos of a crisis with order. It is far more healthy emotionally for our loved ones to use denial than to be panic-stricken.

HOW WE ARE RELEASED FROM SHOCK

Neither denial nor panic can be sustained emotionally. The question, "What has happened?" soon gets translated into a question of anguish, "Why has this happened to me?"

We are released from shock either by the ventilating or withholding of emotions. Freud observed accurately that whatever experiences we have are incorporated into our unconscious and will be expressed overtly in some form of behavior. To put it another way—whatever emotionally goes down has to come up. We can't dispose of emotional upset simply by ignoring it and pretending nothing has happened.

When denial has been used, even with partial success, to muster enough courage to face change, the patient can begin to externalize emotions. It may take some form of emotion such as grief or anger. Whatever the form, it is a catharsis. To be able to cry, for example, is to recognize that our emotional systems, like our bloodstreams, have to be purified. As one patient put it, "When I cry, I am emptying my emotional bladder and it brings as real a relief as elimination."

It is not always easy for health care workers, friends, and family to distinguish between a patient's catharsis and panic. Unlike the cries of panic which indicate that patients fear they might be out of control, however, catharsis is used to recover composure, and as such, it is easily distinguishable by its consequent release.

Unfortunately we may be so unnerved by a patient's catharsis that we project our own feelings of near panic. Sometimes visitors become very uncomfortable when they find their loved ones crying, and they will try to make them stop. In such a case, I ask them if they think they would cry under similar circumstances. Almost always they answer, "yes." Still, they may be unnerved by seeing "my patient" or "my friend" purging his or her emotions. How emotion is expressed is determined largely by what the culture permits, but emotions will be expressed in some way as the person in shock adapts to change.

When emotion is not expressed openly, either because of individual internal controls or because of society's expectations, anger is turned upon one's self as guilt, and release from shock is expressed as depression. It is as though the patient sees crisis as punishment justly applied. I use the word *depression* as a description of the sense of particularized loss of worth: "I deserve what has happened to me." I am well aware of the word's strict usage in psychiatry, but as used there it is impossible to make the needed distinction with *despair*, which will be mentioned later.

When Mrs. A, a woman in her 50s, was diagnosed with Hodgkin's disease, she struggled with real courage to make sense of her situation. She was particularly susceptible to crying following chemotherapy. She would think about the very active life she had led, a life filled with service to others, and think of all that was left to do. She would think of her family who, even though strong and independent in their own ways, were in other ways very dependent on her. "You know, I realize how much people have depended on me when I see how those things that I used to do simply don't get done any more," she said. "I don't want to die. I am still very much needed here."

When she was quiet she was depressed, and her friends and family taxed their abilities in trying to elevate her mood. They behaved as though somehow her depression was a figment of imagination or breakdown of her mind. They kept telling her, "Your disease is arrested. You're OK now. Your worries are all in your head." She had to put up with comments such as these, even though her physical condition had been altered greatly by the disease, she had to go through all of the complications of her therapy every six weeks, and she no longer had the energy to do any more than to move from bed to a chair. When she tried to talk about the things that were most important to her, she would sometimes cry, only to be told by them, "Stop it! Don't you dare cry!" She was caught in a double bind. She was neither supposed to be depressed nor was she permitted to cathart. She was thwarted in her feelings as she attempted to be released from the conflict generated by her question, "Why me?"

Both relatives and health care personnel need to learn how to respect depression. As one patient suffering from cervical cancer put it, "How inappropriate it is for the physician to come in and tell me, 'Depression is not allowed on my ward,' as though somehow or another I do not have a right to grieve over the loss that I am feeling. When I feel blue, I have a right to feel blue. It is appropriate to feel blue." Only as patients are permitted to grieve can they be expected to have the confidence to face change. Many patients long ago discovered how they can best externalize deep emotional conflict. It is important for us to give both opportunity and assurance to patients that emotions can be externalized in ways they feel are appropriate and relieving.

Patient anger because of illness or accident is neither unusual nor inappropriate. It is the recognition that they have sustained real loss. Patients will wrangle, "Why me?" or "Why did I let this happen?" Most patients gain release from shock in both catharsis and depression. Rather than being abnormal, a patient's short-term depression is appropriate. If a patient did not become depressed at times, it would be uncharacteristic behavior. Hopefully though, patients can be assisted to externalize their anger so that the periods of depression become shorter and less severe. To ask, "Why me?" is the second step we take naturally when we are forced by health crisis to change. For patients to keep their sense of dignity, though, they must work "out," not keep "in," feelings of anger, guilt, and disillusionment.

The same emotional dynamics apply to those of us who must adjust to health crises of a loved one. If your family has not openly shared both joy and sorrow, you may fear that externalizing your true feelings will either be rejected as inappropriate by your friends and the health care staff or add an unnecessary burden to the patient. You, too, should ventilate your feelings, sometimes even publicly, so that your periods of depression can become shorter and less severe.

How We Try to Make Sense of Unwanted Change

We try to make sense of unwanted change by worrying about ourselves, by reassessing who and where we are in our world. We may not be as systematic in our measurements as was Benjamin Franklin, who reported that he went through a checklist every night to catch his errors. It is natural, however, to reassess who we are when we realize "things have changed."

For a patient, assessment represents the attempt to answer the questions, "What has happened to me?" "What does this all mean?" and "What's left of me?" Assessment is the attempt to readjust one's identity as a result of new and altering experiences. Crisis and illness alter the context for living, making patients ask, "Who am I now?" Patients who perceive themselves as radically altered, with relationships ruptured, often have difficulty with personal reconciliation. If they have perceived themselves as guilty of some wrongdoing, is it possible to understand being forgiven? If they have been acting out fears of being abandoned, is it possible to be reunited? These are the kinds of concerns with which patients wrestle as they try to assess *where* they are in an apparent attempt to rediscover *who* they are.

Assessing oneself raises many questions, and most patients need encouragement to ask them. It is not too difficult to distinguish between questions that seek data and questions that attempt to assess self-worth. Questions that seek data will be focused: "Why can't I get up?" "Why didn't you get here earlier?" "When is my next dose of medication?" These questions should be answered, if possible. Questions that attempt to assess self-worth tend to be more remote: "What do you think has happened to me?" "Do you think I'm feeling any better?" "Do you think I'm going to last very long?" Behind these spoken questions are hidden suspicions: "Will they listen to my real fears?"

Patients test our reactions to questions. If we are to encourage patients to articulate their suspicions about self-worth, we need to refrain from rendering opinions as an immediate response. We can assure them of the appropriateness of asking questions and discussing suspicions by responding acceptingly with a question in turn: "How does it seem to you?" Patients then may share their true feelings.

Hope, which centers on fulfilling expectations, may focus on getting well, but more often focuses on what yet can be done. It is expressed as having the chance to "finish my business," which may refer to putting financial affairs in order or, as in lengthy illness, a desire for a quick end. In some illnesses, patients have only one hope: "All I want is to control this pain." Sometimes hope is based on a possible miracle that will reverse the degenerating character of illness. Most often, however, patients hope that they will be able to maintain a sense of dignity no matter what. Hope is a perspective and an assessment of what one can expect personally. Staff and relatives mistakenly may hear this expression of hope as denial rather than accommodation to reality.

When we hear a patient say, "I just don't seem to love life anymore," he or she is depressed. When we hear a patient say, "All life is tragic, why do I have to endure it?" it is a sign of despair. Symptoms of despair appear when depression is sustained and the factors that have depressed the patient have become diffuse and generalized. No longer is it just the self that seems to be out-of-joint, but all of life. Despair is the abandonment of hope. It is succumbing to the assessment that there is no more purpose to living. Unlike hope, which seems to be based on patient expectation to locate the self, despair seems to be based on the inability to find a perspective. There is a sense of being cut off, of being alienated.

Max, a patient with AIDS-related problems, expressed both hope and despair during his terminal illness. At first, it seemed that no matter what was being done for him, he was anxious—not in a hostile sort of way, but he was always very tense. When I talked with him he would look past my shoulder. One day I commented, "Max, you seem to be looking for someone or something."

"I do?" he responded. "I wonder who?"

"But you keep looking?"

"Yes."

"There's some reason; can you tell me?"

"I don't know. It's just that nothing seems to make sense anymore."

"Are you hunting for a friend?" I asked.

"No."

"A relative?"

"I don't have any!"

"Are you hunting for your physician?"

"I don't know. I think he was here already."

Checking with his physician, I found he had had the same experience. When he came to see Max, or when the nurses came to give him a bath or to distribute his medications, he looked past them as though he was waiting for something to happen or someone to come. The same thing occurred when his friends came to visit, and he could never determine who or what he was looking for. He was cut off from something, but he knew not what. The more the patient distanced himself, the more his friends and the staff tended to regard him as an object, thereby reinforcing his loss of self-worth. They talked about Max in front of him as though he weren't present. His despair became their alienation.

One day the patient's demeanor changed and he no longer seemed overly anxious. I asked him, "What is it that has changed for you?" I was surprised at his answer. Max said, "Now I know how I'm going to die. I don't have to worry anymore." He did not say, "Now I know that I'm *not* going to die; I don't have to worry about dying." That was not his concern. He was anxious to know how he was going to die so he could prepare for it. Now he knew. He had accepted his terminal condition. He was no longer anxious. Health care staff could tell him about what he could expect. He instructed his friends how to help him put affairs in order. Adaptation for Max did not come easily, but his despair was broken and his anxiety relieved. That didn't mean he was well, but it did mean, "I can cope with life. I can handle my disease. I can make sense out of it. I'm worth the effort."

Assessment represents the kind of tensions that must be resolved when crisis has passed the first wave of intensity and we have time to reflect on who we are. We can do several things to assist patient struggles for self-assessment:

First, we can help them sort through thoughts, in their own time and ways, to help them determine just what resources and strengths they have left. Patients cannot make realistic assessments if the significant people around them resist answering their questions. The excuse, "We haven't told him anything about his condition," or "We don't want to take her hope away from her," both erroneously suppose that patients are asking for all possible information about their situations and that the only ground for hope is to be cured. To the contrary, most patients will limit their questions to the amount of information they are prepared to handle, and many patients, after working through initial disappointment, will find hope even in the willingness of friends, relatives, and health care workers to treat them as functioning, competent adults.

Second, when patients exhibit symptoms of despair, it is often therapeutic to encourage them to be as specific as possible about their feelings. Focused, they can grasp and confront their crises. Generalized and diffused, they cannot make an orderly assessment about themselves because their lives seem chaotic. A patient in despair should have the assistance of someone trained in dynamic therapy—a clinically trained chaplain, social worker, clinical psychologist, psychiatric nurse, or psychiatrist.

THINGS TO AVOID AS WE CHANGE

Being in shock, finding release through ventilation of emotions, and reassessing one's sense of worth represent the ways patients adapt to change. We adapt to change the same way. We, too, must respect our sense of dignity or we may be unable to provide patients with the comfort and support they seek. Because our rate of adaptation may not be the same as the patient's, or because we may need to deny that the patient's health crisis has forced basic change upon us, we may begin to feel that there is nothing we can do. Either we are still in shock or we think the health care personnel can provide all that the patient needs. If we are not careful, we succumb to the "waiting vulture syndrome," which occurs either when we refuse to respect our own emotions or when our mourning in anticipation of loss precedes the death of a patient.

Inez and her family were typical of this syndrome. Inez was a 43-year-old mother of two who was readmitted to the hospital with advanced cancer of the colon. Exploratory surgery found that her colon was totally blocked and that her cancer was spreading rapidly and widely. The patient, like her family, had come into the hospital fully expecting that her disease could be corrected by some medical procedure. Two previous admissions, with surgery, had relieved her cancer symptoms.

When Inez was told that her condition was inoperable, she responded to the physician with the rhetorical question, "Then that means that this will be my last hospitalization, won't it?" The physician was direct but not blunt in confirming her suspicion. Inez was emotionally shocked for a brief period of time, but after a similarly brief period of crying, set herself to the immediate task of getting her affairs in order.

The patient was quiet, articulate, and fully in command of her senses. At no time from the point of admission until she died was she without the presence of at least one member of her family. To the casual observer, to most of the staff, and to many of her relatives, she had a very strong ego. She played a strong role in family affairs. With her husband, however, she exhibited a dependent personality, enduring his alcoholism and promiscuity with countless rhythms of martyred feelings, forgiveness, and reconciliation.

Her husband fled from the hospital upon receiving the physician's diagnosis and was found the following day in a tavern. Her children went into deep shock and had difficulty functioning during the hospitalization. Several of the in-laws assisted Inez by running errands, collecting legal papers, and making telephone calls for her.

On the second day, most of the family spent their time between crying in the hallway and taking turns being in the patient's room. The male members of the family had begun to concern themselves with three questions: (1) "Are we doing all that can be done to help her cope with her suffering?" (2) "How much more time is there?" and (3) "Is it all right to begin making 'final arrangements'?" To the first question, several of the hospital's staff gave sympathetic encouragement by suggesting ways the family could help. To the second question, the physicians and staff were noncommittal as to the precise time that death could be expected, but noted Inez's physical condition continued to deteriorate rapidly. To the third question, the staff encouraged them to "make arrangements" as rapidly as they felt competent.

On the third day after diagnosis, Inez had a siege of vomiting so violent the staff expected her to die at any time. Her mind remained oriented, but focused on the single concern of how to be comfortable. Between bouts of nausea, Inez would concern herself with healing ruptures in family affairs and would call estranged members of the family together at bedside. By the end of the fourth day, she seemed ready to die and informed me, "I think all of my business is finished now." The family had, by and large, expressed their grief less frequently and for shorter periods of time. They had completed legal, financial, and funeral arrangements.

On the fifth day, Inez revived dramatically. She had ceased vomiting and was mentally so alert that she reported on the emotional and physical conditions of all her family with the same kind of detail she shared about herself. She was so bright in spirits that she was telling all who would listen, "I think I'll be going home again."

The relatives were physically and emotionally drained. They stood in the hallway and in the patient's room manifesting the physical characteristics of waiting vultures: drooped heads, shoulders falling forward, listlessness. Emotionally they seemed despondent and resigned. "There's nothing more we can do." They became increasingly angry; first with Inez, then with the staff, and finally with themselves. They expressed their hostilities toward the patient by avoiding eye contact with her, by not responding verbally to her comments and questions, and by long absences from her room. As one of her brothers blurted out, "If she's going to die, why doesn't she go ahead and die?" Then he quickly controlled himself and said, "I don't really mean that. I want her to live, but not if she's going to be eaten up with cancer some more." The family also expressed feelings about how the staff had "misled" them into thinking Inez was going to die. The staff had encouraged them to make "final arrangements." Now what would people think of them? What would Inez think of them if she ever found out? What were they to think of themselves? They felt guilty and angry for precipitously acting out their sense of loss when they were told that she was dying.

Many of the staff were very uncomfortable with the turn of events. They had expected Inez to continue going through the "stage all terminally ill patients are supposed to move," as a nurse put it. "Now she's out of sync!" They were embarrassed by the patient's failure to conform to preconceived ideals of terminal illness and by the relatives' hostility. "We thought we were really doing everything so well."

By the end of the day, Inez felt very estranged, and said so. "It's as though I've become some sort of pariah. I'm being rejected because I'm not dying! Am I no longer a human being?" The relatives seemed unable to respond: "What more can we do? We've done everything we know how to do!" Thinking they could best support the relatives by agreeing, the staff assured them they had done everything they could. But they had not done everything.

One of the goals of professional care is to help patients, relatives, and health care personnel learn how to adapt to the realities of dying and to utilize their resources of grieving in order to cope with loss. Appearance of the waiting vulture syndrome is a sign of both success and failure. It is the sign of success because it indicates that those afflicted have begun to process and express their sense of loss. It is a sign of failure, however, because it exposes those afflicted to the sense that they have precipitously accommodated themselves to a loss, and therefore leads one to assume that there is no more relationship possible with a loved one before death occurs. Feelings of helplessness ("there's nothing more we can do") are coupled with feelings of guilt ("we're ready too soon").

The error of the hospital staff was not their encouragement of the family to make "final arrangements," but rather their reinforcing the feelings of the family that "we've done everything we can." Even for patients who are unconscious, it is important that relatives continue to show affection and assurance that they won't abandon them. Holding their hands, brushing their hair, and massaging their arms and legs are ways of maintaining contact. This also applies to patients who seemingly no longer recognize friends and relatives. The waiting vulture syndrome disappeared as soon as Inez's family began to show her affection and reinvest themselves in *her* welfare.

When Inez died on the eighth day after diagnosis, she died with a sense of ease. Several times during her final hour, she thanked those around her for their presence. She remained conscious until about 15 minutes before her death. The relatives and staff seemed genuine in the self-assessment after her death: "We *did* do everything we could."

For Inez and her family, dying meant radical change. When Inez or her relatives tried pretending that they were not changed, they became alienated in their pretense. However, when they were honest to themselves and each other, and when they expressed their true emotions of anger, guilt, and bewilderment, they were freed to also express their emotions of affection, thankfulness and solace. Rather than dying being the occasion of alienation, for them it became the opportunity to reaffirm their relationships.

It is my observation that no matter what the circumstances of dying may be, we are able to cope providing we have sufficient time to process feelings stimulated by loss and are given the presence of persons who model affirming and adaptive behavior. If we try to pretend we aren't changed by dying, we become alienated in our pretense. If, however, we can ventilate our emotions of anger, guilt, and bewilderment, we can begin realistic self-assessment that permits us to maintain our sense of dignity although our troubles lie heavy upon us.

4

When Dying Means Conflict

Knowledge puffs up, but love builds up.
1 Corinthians 8:1

Interpersonal conflict can be more upsetting than fears of death or pain of disease, particularly for those of us who try to avoid combative relationships. Few of us would will to do anything other than "the right thing" for a patient, yet a clash of opinion, competition with other "helpers," and differences of perspective can easily become occasions for emotional battles. All of us who are acquainted with the patient assume that we know the patient's needs. But our knowledge is not always consistent with the patient's perspective or based on the facts of the patient's crisis.

The bizarre struggle over interpretation of Carl's needs was unusual only in the length of time it took for death to end the matter. Carl, a tall, slender, five-year-old, was admitted unconscious to a hospital emergency room on a hot summer day. He had been hit on the fore-head in a teeter-totter accident at a nearby nursery school. His vital signs were unstable and his eyes had dilated markedly. There were strong indications of brain stem damage, which would endanger proper functioning of his major organs.

Throughout the 15 days of Carl's hospitali-zation, his mother was cold, demanding, and overly anxious. Her demeanor fluctuated be-tween expressions of guilt and feelings of an-ger. Little or no affection was expressed about the boy. Yet, when told that the patient's con-dition was hopeless, she would assert: "He'll be all right!" And she made this a demand on the physician.

Despite the advice of two neurosurgical con-sultants, the physician put the boy on a res-pirator and administered medication for sus-taining vital signs. The physician frequently exploded at the nursing staff, warning them that if the boy died, "I will be sued, and you will be too!" He repeatedly changed orders and demanded excessive testing. He seemed, to everyone concerned, to be equally anxious about legal repercussions and his own fears of dying. "I cannot fail to keep this boy alive. I cannot let death win," became his obsession. Carl had no father. From every indicator to which the staff had access, Carl's mother was a nurturing and competent woman—except in this crisis.

After 15 days of heroic efforts, the patient's heart failed and could not be revived. Autopsy confirmed what the neurosurgeons, nurses, and observers suspected 14 days previous: the thinking part of the boy's brain died soon after hospitalization. Through the use of heroic efforts, certain vital signs were sustained for an extended period. But even life-preserving equipment cannot keep some tissues vital. As some tissues began to decompose, the nursing staff had to work with a corpse that gave off an increasingly strong odor. But for whose benefit? "Each of us felt that the care plan was being cruel to Carl," the head nurse reported. "We felt he should have the right to die in peace." Carl's mother, nurses, and physicians each claimed to be the patient's advocate. All justified themselves by saying, "I know what he needs," when they really were concerned with something more than the patient's needs.

I am sometimes asked by relatives, "If everyone wants to do the right things for patients, how can there be conflict?" It is a troubling question. Some people try to answer it in sweeping anger at hospitals and health care staffs: "Everyone should be allowed to die at home," as if the home setting is free of conflict for a patient. Others have argued that conflict arises as a result of ignorant behavior: "Only professional staff know how to care adequately for a patient," as though training makes professional persons the only experts about a given patient's emotional needs. Even family members, functioning more out of their sense of anxiety and guilt, have mixed motives.

My own answer is based on my understanding of anxiety. When we are anxious about a patient's health crisis—and even experts are when a patient is critically or terminally ill—we become all the more concerned about our own behavior. The more anxious we become, the more we tend to attempt hiding our anxieties by appearing knowledgeable about the patient. We try to hide fears that we may not be doing the right thing or we may not be doing all we can. I have been called as a consultant on a number of occasions when competition and conflict were so intense it never occurred to the combatants to consult the conscious patient about personal needs.

In our own anxiety about other people's health crises, we tend to make their needs our own and we then try to meet patient needs in ways that we have learned may resolve our own emotional crises. Unfortunately, our ways often are not the ways of the patient. The following six examples are intended to show how differently people try to resolve emotional crises; such differences are the basis for much of the conflict that occurs in health crises.

HERBERT AND DARLENE

Herbert and Darlene lived all of their lives in the southeastern part of the United States. They had no living children. Now that they were in their late 50s, they had drawn more and more into themselves emotionally and had only the smallest circle of friends. While bathing one evening, Darlene noticed a lump in her breast and suspected that it might be malignant. Her mother and several other relatives had died of cancer. Darlene shared her discovery with Herbert, but any motivation she might have had to see a physician was squelched by his response: "If you're going to have cancer, there's nothing we can do about it!" She did not visit a physician until the pain of an open lesion forced her to seek relief.

When the physician told the couple that there was nothing that could be done surgically, the couple showed no emotional reaction. They acted as though their suspicions

were confirmed: "If you're going to have cancer, there's nothing we can do about it!" They
had risked conflict at all costs, using what appeared to be passive strength to fight for control. They returned home and continued res-
olutely to carry on their lives' rituals without
deviation. They displayed no emotions of en-
thusiasm or anguish. They preferred to trade
away medical care for uninvolvement, honesty
for quietness, and love for a truce. Their stoicism could not tame pain, however. The more
Darlene needed Herb's affection to counter-
balance her suffering, the more he withdrew
from her. Her dying meant the worst of trag-
edies to him, and his defense was withdrawal.
He expected his crisis to be avoided by emotional stoicism. The conflict they both had tried
to avoid was now inevitable.

REBECCA

Rebecca was a patient in an intensive care unit.
She had received severe burns in a home accident. Over 60 years of age, she was the
mother of five children, and was very devout
in her faith. Even though immense pain occurs
with her kind of accident, she remained calm,
undemanding, and pleasant. The nurses kept

saying to each other, "She must need pain medication," but they never asked her. They were too much in awe of her serenity. Only after death did they learn from the family of her immense suffering.

Rebecca had seen her situation as part of life's mixture of temptation and righteousness. She thought of her behavior as being judged. She had been preparing for such a crisis most of her life. In the fight between good and evil, she was prepared to assume full responsibility for maintaining a good battle. When asked by the family if she was in pain, she had exclaimed, "Oh yes, this is a real test of my faith, but I'll win." The family understood the context for such a witness of faith. To them, dying was the final and ultimate test of their religious beliefs. Consequently, they did not interfere on her behalf to ask for additional pain medication. That would have been a sign of weakness. They expected to overcome crisis by tenacious faith and serenity.

Unfortunately, patients with this kind of personality trait seem to be the most neglected patients in health-care centers because their emotions either are misdiagnosed or misunderstood. Frequently, those who cannot believe that there can be a genuinely serene personality will define the patient as "stoical," "overly dependent," or maintaining "mass denial." In either their hostility toward religion or their misunderstanding of the power of religious faith, staff may interpret behavior like Rebecca's as bizarre, peculiar, inappropriate, and even impossible.

DOCTOR JOHN

Doctor John was a well-respected physician in his community. He exhibited all of those characteristics that give impressions of self-control, competence, efficiency, thoroughness, and principled behavior. Unfortunately, Dr. John could not handle emotional problems, particularly those surrounding a dying patient. He looked on dying patients as living proof of his failure as a physician.

Like other people who, in times of crisis, emphasize law over grace, ideals over accommodation, and justice over forgiveness, Dr. John became very moralistic with patients who were critically and terminally ill. He made it sound, when he talked at all, that the patient wouldn't be experiencing the crisis if he didn't somehow deserve it. Dying—for him—was a moral judgment. It called into question not only the righteousness of the patient, but the competence of the physician.

Beliefs in human perfectibility and the life of the mind tend to drive one toward mastery of thought processes and dominion of thoughts over feelings in order to guarantee preconceived avoidance. In times of crises, spontaneity is thwarted and rhythms of living are transformed into inflexible rituals of orderliness. Several theories try to explain this behavior trait, but it is widely assumed that these people have the feeling that they are loved not because of their inherent worth, but because of their good works. "I have to be perfect if I am to be loved," they say.

Persons like Dr. John are found in disproportionate numbers among health care professions. One reason they enter their profession seems to be the need to overcome feelings of inadequacy, especially in the face of dying. Some health-care workers check their fears by being efficient, so they expect patients to handle their anxieties in the same way. The more a patient became chaotic or ambiguous, the more obsessed Dr. John became with orderliness and efficiency.

MARILYN

Marilyn, a 50-year-old homemaker, had lived her whole life in a midwestern rural community. Her only interests were those of her family. Between caring for her home in early mornings and late evenings, she did heavy chores. She had no interests or hobbies of her own. Always, she worked for her family. Marilyn's husband and children would discuss politics and current events at the table, but she seldom if ever rendered an opinion, and only then, after she was sure of her husband's stance. When she was diagnosed with cancer of the cervix, she was not informed of the diagnosis on orders from her family. Even after the disease had spread widely and she had been hospitalized, her family regularly lectured the staff about the necessity of keeping her diagnosis a secret.

Marilyn's husband and children first channeled their energies into making up games to play with her. They established schedules for her in the near future for parties, clubs, and circle meetings, few of which she had ever attended when she had been well. The family members acted as though they were in complete control of every situation, and they were—except over the disease. They insisted that Marilyn be given some drug or perhaps electric shock therapy so that she "wouldn't have to worry." They said they didn't want her "to be burdened." Under their relentless prodding, both the attending physician and Marilyn agreed to shock therapy. When asked whether she would approve of such treatment, she told the therapist, "I guess I'll do anything to make my family comfortable." That had been the way she had always handled conflict.

Marilyn's family exhibited hyperindependence characterized by attempts to control feelings for fear of showing their weaknesses. Unlike Dr. John, described in the example above, Marilyn's family avoided frustration by refusing to look at illness or dying. Instead of focusing feelings of guilt or inadequacy on themselves, they blamed others. Marilyn was made to adjust her feelings for their needs to the point that Marilyn couldn't even identify her feelings. The family's sense of independence was exaggerated. No regulation of the hospital or procedure of care was left unchallenged. They brought friends to see Marilyn, but if they became emotionally dependent in a way that they threatened the family's hyperindependence, the friends were rejected. Marilyn's dying meant loss to them, but more significantly, their feelings of helplessness meant that their attempts to be independent were called into question. The family reacted with callous denial in their attempt to maintain a sense of autonomy.

Marilyn related to her family's hyperindependence with overdependent behavior. She avoided asking questions about her situation and responded to questions in ways she thought she was expected to answer. While her own dying was painful to her, her basic conflict was fear of rejection if she exhibited independent behavior or opinions.

MRS. B

Mrs. B was a 45-year-old mother who became the frequent focus for comment by the hospital staff when she took up residency at the time her son was admitted. He was a patient in the acute care unit for leukemia patients. Mrs. B's husband showed some emotion about their son's condition, but never appeared to make any of the decisions concerning his treatment. Mrs. B was very demanding with the nurses, but when one of the male physicians or interns came into her son's room, she would quickly change her demeanor into that of a coquettish, helpless little girl. She tried to "baby" her 26-year-old son, saying things such as, "Now get well for Mommy, so Mommy can be happy again," or, "You are really making Mommy feel very tired keeping me at the hospital all of the time." At other times, she would blame her son's condition on her husband's neglect, the son's neglect, or their family physician, whom she now termed "an incompetent quack." She was never interested in the details of her son's illness or in any explanations of why he was not recovering. When it was obvious that her son was dying, she cried copiously—for herself, it seemed.

Mrs. B was very impulsive. Unlike Marilyn, described in the example above, Mrs. B used her dependency as a means to control others. Self-indulgent, emotionally unstable, and overreactive, she used hysterics to get her way. She seemed never to be able to develop mature, trusting relationships. In place of having a sense of confidence or a sense of responsibility, she always tried to seek out an ideal person, a father-figure who would protect her and who would solve all of her problems. She often used means of seductiveness and helplessness to find such a person.

Because of her easy suggestibility, the hospital staff tried to minimize conflict by giving her few details of her son's illness. While they met her direct questions honestly, firmly, and patiently, they wisely avoided elaborating. The statements the staff did make were exaggerated when used by Mrs. B in attempts to manipulate feelings of guilt or sympathy in people around her.

What her son's health crisis meant to her was revealed in her tantrum when he was pronounced dead. She jumped from her chair and rushed to his bedside screaming: "You have failed me! You have failed me! I am very angry with you!" But it was not her son, but the means she had come to trust for handling crisis, that failed her.

MR. R

Mr. R was a 75-year-old man whose wife had been admitted to the hospital with congestive heart failure. She was also diagnosed as "senile." While Mr. R manifested some characteristics of senility himself, his hostile behavior was consistent with what his relatives could recall about him as far back as they could remember. When approached by members of the hospital staff, friends or relatives, he would accuse them of plotting against him and his wife. He appeared to everyone around him as self-centered, rigid, childish, and generally hostile. When he succeeded in driving most people away from him, he accused everybody of abandoning him in his hour of need, thereby confirming his most vivid suspicions about "this whole rotten world." Relatives were accused of coming to visit only to court favor for inheritance purposes. Physicians were accused of rendering no service but grabbing more money. Even his wife was failing him by dying first. Ridiculing and taunting, testing and reproving, he alienated himself from everyone, blaming them for what was missing in himself.

Hostility may take either active or passive forms. When active, people like Mr. R tend to explode emotionally as a standard reaction to new experiences and appear confirmed in the belief that they are victims of some conspiracy. When passive, they show their hostility in passive-aggressive pouting, stubbornness, or refusal to cooperate with care plans. Mr. R used hostility to try to prevent change until he could adjust—a painfully slow process for him. Now, with his deep feelings of loneliness, he was determined that he would be needed by his wife until she died. By driving most people away from his wife's room, he succeeded. At the same time, however, his fears of having to continue living as a disgruntled, lonely old man were reinforced.

As a word of caution to the reader, it is important to distinguish between individuals whose anger and hostility are characteristic of pre-aging personalities and those who exhibit the symptoms as a result of disease. If hostility has not been part of the individual's personality, it is then important to distinguish between organic and situational origins. Organic origins need to be determined by a physician. Most situational origins, however, such as bad care, failure to be listened to, or abandonment, can usually be corrected by demonstrated concern and affection.

REDUCING CONFLICT

These six examples are intended to show how our perspective of the patient's health crises and our expectations about appropriate ways of handling them may be incompatible with other people's expectations and ways. It is so easy, particularly in times of crises, to generalize our own perspectives and thereby to assume unwarranted knowledge of the patient's situation. When a physician handles her anxiety by trying to be efficient at the time relatives are ambiguous about how to proceed with the patient's care; when a husband handles his anxiety by distancing himself emotionally just when his wife needs frequent affection for reassurance; when a patient handles her anxiety by verbalizing anger and hostility; when her relatives handle anxiety by repressing emotions, conflict is the result.

For most of us—relatives, friends, staff, or patient—interpersonal conflict is more troublesome than the inner struggles we have with feelings of pain, grief, and ambiguity, now made particularly intense because "time is running out."

What can be done to reduce conflict? No one knows all that can be known about patient needs—not even a spouse of 50 years or an eminent physician. Consequently, it is important, for both patients and those who care for them, that as broad a spectrum of perspectives as possible be available for designing a patient care plan. That spectrum of perspectives should include family members, health care professionals, and patients. The patients, however, must be the principal evaluators of what is appropriate or inappropriate care. It is their sense of dignity that is the measure by which our help must be judged; not our feelings, not our relationships with the patients, not our professional roles.

When we begin to have interpersonal conflicts, we can do several things to reduce them. First, we can stop and ask ourselves what is behind our own feelings. Perhaps we have some feelings of guilt about our prior relationships with a particular patient. Perhaps we feel inadequate to meet our loved one's health crises.

If so, a second thing we can do is ask for assistance for ourself, working through our own inner conflicts with someone sympathetic. Our pastor, a social worker, a hospital chaplain, or a friend may be appropriate.

Third, we need to communicate with other members of the family and the health care team, not in a combative or hostile way, but in ways that our own perspective can be of help when planning for patient care. We have a right to know what we can expect from others and an obligation to find out what they expect of us.

Fourth, we need to be open to the variety of ways emotions are expressed in health crises. Contrary to the way we may believe, and despite the way we may behave, our own emotional involvement with the patient usually prevents us from being very knowledgeable. On the one hand, we must rely on health care personnel for much of the knowledge needed in the patient's physical care precisely because they are not as emotionally involved. On the other hand, an expert's systematic application of knowledge may be neat and orderly and yet be utterly oppressive to the patient because it does not address the problem the patient feels. We need to address the patient at the level of the patient's own feelings.

Fifth, love for the patient should have our highest priority, even above some knowledgeable opinion, or concept of professional role, or sense of ethics. "Knowledge puffs up, but love builds up." Love even overcomes conflict.

5

When Dying Means Suffering

So teach us to number our days, that we
may apply our hearts unto wisdom.
Psalm 90:12 KJV

Why do human beings suffer? Perhaps no other question has been wrestled with more persistently in human history than this one. The persistence and pervasiveness of suffering, however, have not kept us from believing that happiness should be normative for living. Suffering, we believe, ought not belong to life.

High expectations are placed on medical science. If, for some reason, suffering does occur, people expect physicians to prescribe a cure-all. If a cure-all is not possible, a pain killer will do. Modern medicine has given us considerable control over many forms of pain, but it is not uncommon to discover that even when pain is relieved, suffering remains.

Loneliness, guilt, conflict—these and more are the elements of suffering. When suffering occurs, our natural inclination is to ask, "Why? Why me?" We question not only the phenomenon of the moment but the very nature of our existence.

Al was a 50-year-old laborer from a blue-collar suburb of Chicago. He was admitted to a metropolitan hospital after being diagnosed with cancer of the liver. He was visited frequently by most members of his family and a few friends even though the hospital was far from home. Al's disease was inoperable, but he did not seem to be in great pain. Yet, although staff and family were meeting his physical needs, he suffered greatly. He resisted talking about his feelings with his friends, but he was quite open with members of the health care staff. "Why?" he asked over and over. "Why should I be suffering?"

OCCASIONS FOR SUFFERING

The question, "Why me?" indicates that Al was suffering because he believed his hopes and expectations were being violated. Al had never planned to suffer. He had been active at work and at home until a month before his hospitalization. He had little warning of his health crisis. He was not prepared for any diagnosis as grave as the one he received. He was happily married and the father of two daughters and a son. He was active in the men's organization of his church. He enjoyed companionship with the people in his community. He and his wife, Erma, had worked hard and in doing so they were about to make the last payment on their house mortgage. They had been able to provide their children with more material goods than they themselves had in their youth, and they were well on the road to setting aside sufficient income for a comfortable retirement. The diagnosis of cancer simply was not in Al's plans.

When his physician shared the test results with him, Al's first reaction was disbelief. "Surely some mistake has been made." He became angry at the physician. "How could he do this to me?" Al sought an examination from a second physician, but the original diagnosis was confirmed. Still, Al couldn't believe this was happening to him. "If the diagnosis is true," he thought, "all the careful planning that Erma and I have done is for nothing." Life had become meaningless.

Al suffered for another reason. While it was not the official teaching of his religion, he, like many of his friends, believed that disease is punishment for wrongdoing. Those who lived righteously, he believed, were rewarded with prosperity, good health, and longevity. When suffering occurred it was because the sufferer, or one of his relatives, had been immoral, Al believed. And premature death was punishment for sins, overt or concealed, sometimes unknown even to those who commit them. How could he, a good man, now be suffering? The conflict violated his sense of logic and his notion of consistency.

Yet a third occasion of Al's suffering came as a consequence of the conflict between the person he thought he ought to be and the person who now felt so impotent. How was he to be the man he was supposed to be? The conflict offended his sense of propriety.

OCCASIONS FOR RELEASE FROM SUFFERING

Al struggled with his question, "Why me?" and in doing so began to reassess his expectations. He had always pictured himself as dying quickly—in an accident or from a heart attack. His family would mourn his death but there would be, in his mind's eye, no pain and no suffering. As he adapted to the realities of his illness, he seemed to give up being offended by the fact that his dying would be a lingering process. This approach, in itself, brought no relief to his suffering.

Al found real comfort in the regular visits by his wife and daughters. After one visit, he began to reminisce about the people and the things that were most important to him. He joked about his adventures in traveling all over the country when he was young and single, but it was his life as a father that he most treasured. When I asked him to name the things that were his most important achievements, his answers centered around the role of father. He had taught his girls to be modest; he had taught his son how to play ball and how to defend himself. He had taught them how to be honest and how to work hard.

His answers gave me the opportunity to ask, "And what do you have left to teach your son?" His son had never been mentioned except as Al reminisced about the boy's childhood.

Explosively, he reacted to my question: "What son! I don't have a son anymore!" Then he began to cry profusely.

After a while, Al began to speak again. "You know, I've talked about how the most important things in life to me have been in the things I've done as a father. But I've really failed as a father. My son won't let me teach him anything more. I kicked him out last year." Out poured a tale of painful conflict between a father and his teenage son. "You ought to see him! He has hair down to his shoulders."

I asked him, "What is so important about the fact that your son has long hair?"

Incredulous, he asked a rhetorical question, "You know what long hair means in Cicero? It means my son isn't a man. I've failed to raise my son to be a man!" It made little difference to Al that most of his son's friends had similar hair styles or clothes at that time. Al was not persuaded by being told his son would have been rejected by his peer group if he conformed to the styles then popular in a conservative community.

As their conflict stretched out into months, Al and his son were unable to communicate about anything. Their relationship was ruptured. Al interpreted his feelings as the occasion when his son "called the family's good name into question among the neighbors." Now embarrassment had become hard fact. Al understood himself not only to have failed as a father but as the son of his father.

We didn't linger on the subject of styles and teenage behavior very long; that was not the important point. I didn't want to miss the opportunity of calling him back to what he had articulated as the most important expectation he had for himself—the role of teacher. I asked my question again: "Is there something more that you can teach your son?"

Al thought for a while and then replied, "Well, I don't know what it could be."

"Is there such a thing as teaching him how to die well?" I asked. "Is there something about the experience that you're having now that would be valuable for him to know?"

Partial release from his suffering occurred as Al began to reflect on what he could yet give his son. He could use the occasion of his suffering to give his son a last gift.

In Al's desire for reconciliation with his son, he began to release his son as an object of anger. As he discovered that he could forgive his son, Al began to have a change of heart about his notions of retribution. Some suffering, he could see, is the direct consequence of human error. Automobile accidents caused by drunken drivers, farm and industrial accidents that result from careless workers, an infant's injury that occurs while a mother is distracted, are all occasions of suffering as a direct consequence of human behavior. What about terminal illness, though? What about cancer?

Al's physician explained that on the basis of medical research we know that most diseases are not the results of immoral or licentious behavior. In our attempts to find order in the chaos of our health crises, however, we easily draw cause-and-effect conclusions that have little or no bearing on reality. Some people try to explain their suffering by postulation: "It was because of what I did when I was 16," or "I was hit there and became deeply bruised," or "I ate the wrong foods when I was a teenager," or again, "I sowed too many wild oats when I was a youngster." Endless reasons can be given. As do many people, Al did not distinguish between those health crises that come as a direct result of human error and those that are from bodily breakdown.

By distinguishing between what he knew and what he could not know, Al gradually began to release himself from feelings of guilt based on the assumption that somehow, in some way unknown to him, his cancer was the consequence of grievous sins. He had been unwilling to verbalize it, but he feared that his cancer was God's punishment for having failed as a father. He had wondered, too, if his son's errant behavior had brought divine disfavor down upon the family. In his anger, Al had been holding himself accountable for his disease, then his son, and finally God. Now he could be released from his notions of retribution.

Until Al had wrestled with the implications of forgiving and being forgiven, he thought he ought to be the perfect man. As long as he held to the pretense that he had to be a perfect, righteous man if he were to avoid punishment, he had held himself tenaciously to an accountability that neither he nor any other person is able to muster.

It was the Danish philosopher Søren Kierkegaard who reminded people of Al's persuasion that before God we are all failures, and therefore do not have to pretend a "sufferlessness" none of us can attain. Al had believed that if he were anything less than perfect, he would be considered weak, impotent, and inadequate. This, he thought, would make him not only unacceptable to his family, but to God. Yet, secretly, he felt that he was a failure as a father and was about to be found out as his disease progressed. As Al was able to forgive his son and release him to be the man that the son was, Al was able to release himself to be the man that he, himself, truly was.

Al sent a letter to his son requesting that he come to the hospital as soon as possible. It was quite an emotional reconciliation. There were no words about hair. "I have lots to tell you," Al shared. "I need to tell you that I found out what it feels like to be cut off from someone you really love. I think it is more painful to me than this thing that's got me. I also want to give you something. I want to show you that you can still be a man even though you hurt. I want to show you that you can die without being destroyed."

Al died soon after reconciling himself with his son. It was a peaceful death. Like the biblical Job, Al suffered because of the conflict he felt between his expectations for himself and the reality of his health crisis. Ironically, his sense of worth was restored when he discovered that he had not been rejected because he was an imperfect man. He was released from alienation when his loneliness was pierced in the sharing of love with another. His release came not as a result of any good works, but in the awareness that he was accepted even though, in his words, he no longer "worked good."

OCCASIONS FOR ADDRESSING SUFFERING THERAPEUTICALLY

Release from the offense of suffering comes when a person discovers "in the defenselessness of suffering the dissolution of defensiveness."[7] There probably is not one among us who has the insight or ability to avoid occasions for suffering. I do not say that suffering is necessary, but occasions of suffering are a part of life and do force us to reexamine our expectations for life. They also force on us the discovery of our pretensions. When people we love are critically or terminally ill, we suffer. Their pain stimulates our suffering. We may try terribly hard to pretend that we aren't threatened, that we can be strong enough to meet our loved one's every need, that we can be the perfect companion in crisis. But if the truth be told, one of the occasions for a patient's suffering is seeing how the crisis of a person we love causes us pain, and the more we pretend that this is not so, the more defensive we become and the more susceptible we are to reacting with what I have described as the abandonment syndrome or the surrogate suffering syndrome.

Part of our defensiveness is expressed when we refuse to talk with patients about their suffering. In an attempt to "do the right thing" relatives sometimes request that patients not even be told the nature of their crisis.

Marian tried to be a surrogate sufferer for her mother. Marian was a smartly dressed, middle-aged woman. When the diagnostic results became available, she instructed the physician not to tell her mother. The physician wrote the following order on the patient's chart: "Do not inform patient of either her diagnosis or prognosis." In the following days, the patient wondered why no one was saying anything to her about the very reason for which she had come to the hospital. Marian would make bright, guarded conversation as she hovered protectively at bedside, and the physicians and nurses evaded her mother's questions.

Why had Marian insisted that her mother not be informed about her incurable disease? "My mother is a very good woman. She has had to put up with a lot of suffering in her life, most of it inflicted by other people. I'm not going to let her suffer anymore." Ironically, the daughter was reenacting an episode of suffering inflicted on her mother by other people.

I have never informed a patient that he or she is dying. I have never needed to do so. Patients come to a hospital for a reason. They have suspicions, fears, and feelings about being there. If possible, most patients like to leave a hospital as soon as possible with the hope that they can carry on a normal life. The longer they are held in the hospital, the greater the suspicions, fears, and feelings about being there. I suppose there are patients who have been hoodwinked by relatives and staff, but I have yet to meet one. Evasion is a lie, and once you tell a lie, you have to build a care plan around it. Too many people are involved with administering a patient's care plan to maintain effective deceptiveness. Consequently, relatives and physicians who try to keep a diagnosis from a patient usually are frustrated, but not in the way popularly thought.

At the University of Chicago I conducted a study to see how terminally ill patients who had not been told their diagnosis nevertheless seemed to know they had a grim prognosis. Out of a sample of 65 patients, I found the following results: All but one of the terminally ill patients told me that they thought they were dying. The one exception had become comatose before I could complete the study.

I asked each patient, "Why are you here?"

Some patients would first test me to see how I would react to their feelings. That was the way it was with Marian's mother. Then, guardedly, she said, "Well, I think I have a disease I will die from."

"How do you know this?" I asked.

"I don't think I'm supposed to know. My daughter sees to that. But I know. Everyone started acting funny the day I was supposed to hear what was wrong."

Another patient identified the very person who had given the order not to tell as the one who had, in fact, communicated the news to her: "My doctor has always looked me squarely in the eyes when talking to me—until that day. He has not looked at my face since completing his workup of my case. I know the results even though he told me I was going to be fine."

In more than 80 percent of the cases, ironically, the person who had ordered that the diagnosis be kept secret was the one whom the patient identified as having revealed the secret.

Various communication studies indicate that we convey less than 30 percent of our feelings by words. More than 70 percent of our feelings are conveyed through gestures. Patients know relatives and staff better than we know the patient. All of the patient's attention can be focused on our behavior. We usually have other concerns, particularly when we try to keep a secret. So the question is not, "Should we tell the patient?" but, "What is the best way to communicate the diagnosis?"

The attempt to shoulder patients' suffering for them is as futile as to try to do their dying for them. Every attempt to be surrogate sufferers imposes an additional burden of suffering on the patients.

We err when we think that what our loved ones most need from us is that we be perfect, unsuffering, and unfeeling. As one woman put it, "It would be so nice if I could just talk with my husband and children about our common suffering. But we can't. If I indicate that I am suffering, they begin to twitch as though I'm accusing them of neglect. They think they have to be so brave and strong. But the more helpless they really feel, the more pushy they become. That's why I like talking to you. You're nobody to me. I can say what I really feel like saying without fearing unwanted consequences. Still, it would really be a comfort if I could share my feelings with those I love."

Just as patients need someone to help them work through their feelings so they can be released from their questions of self-pity and anger, so we need help discovering the origins of our feelings. As we try to do the right thing for patients, as we try to be the perfect companion, we force ourselves into giving them pretentiousness when what they need is compassion. Who but one who has suffered can know the meaning of compassion?

We suffer because we are mortal. And all schemes for avoiding or eliminating suffering are soon exposed as pious deceits when we, ourselves, suffer. We do not will to suffer. Human suffering is the sole source of personal understanding and insight into the afflictions of others. Suffering can curse our life with bitterness and resentment, but it can also enable us to reach out in sympathetic concern toward another who suffers. The suffering we have in common, then, can be the occasion for a healing relationship of love and acceptance. It is the answer to our prayer "that we may apply our hearts unto wisdom."

6

When Dying Means Triumph

O death, where is thy victory?
O death, where is thy sting?
1 Corinthians 15:55

How can dying ever mean triumph? When I began my career nearly 25 years ago, it never occurred to me that I could write such a chapter as this. The reason I am able to do so is because of the insights shared by my many teachers—the many critically and terminally ill patients, their families, and the health care personnel who served them. Before learning from them, I was skeptical that dying could mean anything other than a horrific, final tragedy that ends everything worthwhile. Either that, or, for life to have meaning, death had to be an illusion.

Dying does mean the end of everything worthwhile to some patients, and other patients fear death so much that they try desperately to believe that life is unending. Dying can be terribly threatening. One woman was quite correct when she warned that it would only be another game of rationalization if we tried "to domesticate death."

For most of us, death and dying are such generalized concepts that we do not know what generates our fears. Not unlike children who are afraid of the dark because they can't focus on the unexperienced, many of us fear dying as an unknown. Given the time to work through their feelings, the overwhelming majority of patients find that they not only could, but did, conquer their fears. While failing to domesticate death, they nevertheless can measure their dying against living rather than living in fear of dying. The overwhelming majority of patients find that they can both affirm their life and acknowledge the realities of their dying. Released from conflict, they can live—and die—in dignity.

WHAT POWER HAS DEATH?

Initially, almost all patients have fears that they cannot cope with dying. They must struggle to put their experience in a perspective they can grasp. "I just didn't expect it to be this way," one man confessed. Patients must discover whether their expectations, beliefs, and values would betray them in their hour of crisis. More importantly, they must discover whether dying will cut them off from the love that has made life worth living.

Some patients discover that rather than trusting the Lord whom they have named in their prayers, they have been obedient through fear to the god, death. Some patients discover that they are so burdened by inherited, corporate guilt, they have been persuaded that death is the ultimate moral power in their lives: "death befalls the wicked" is the commandment of death. Some patients discover that their sense of righteousness is not based on some sharing of love with another or on their sense of morality, but on a belief that their behavior is an insurance policy against insecurity, suffering, and loneliness. They discover that they give much of their lives in unwitting appeasement to death.

Western anthropologists seem to relish identifying taboos of primitive people as though taboos are characteristic only of primitives. But many patients discover that those of us in the "civilized" West also have taboos. For example, consider the never-questioned but obediently served fears of dying. Patient fears shape their emotions, their behavior, and their outlook on life. Like the sting of a farmer's electric fence that keeps cows corralled, these fears keep them imprisoned. This is death's power.

The power of death comes from irrational fears that drive us to pretend that loss is not inherent in living, that suffering is not appropriate for the righteous, that conflict is immoral for the loving—a life not one of us can attain. If we have committed ourselves to a life-style of avoidance, dying then can be the most anxiety-producing experience of our living. This is death's sting. Death has defined our life.

Our Puritan forebears knew well the power of death. In the wilderness of New England they were committed to building a "city on a hill" that could be used as an example of God's will for people around the world. Yet, in their wisdom, even as they proclaimed their allegiance to God—called Jehovah or YHWH by some—the Puritans knew how easily they could be seduced into service to death. Included in their catechism was the question: "If it be the will of the Lord, are you willing to be damned for his glory?" The great commandment of God is: "You shall love the Lord your God with all your heart, and with all your soul, and with all your mind" (Matt. 22:37). If Puritans were not able to answer the catechetical question with a yes, they knew their true allegiance was other than to God. The question reminded them that simply to proclaim obedience does not mean that the heart has been surrendered.

Many patients wrestle with the question of allegiances. They see their struggles as a reenactment, for them, of the cosmological battle between good and evil, between the God of life and the power of death. Some patients speak of struggling with the devil; others, with suffering. Regardless of how they identify their conflict, however, they wrestle with basic questions about human nature.

When we look at ancient Egypt, we see how concerned the pharaohs were with their own struggles against death. The pharaohs considered themselves, by nature, privileged and quite unlike the mortals over whom they ruled. They thought of themselves as gods, and therefore, immortal by definition. Their preparations for protecting themselves against death were most impressive. Yet, as monumental as pyramids are, they stand as revelations of the extremes to which human beings can go in desperate attempts to sandbag our lives against the power of death.

In ancient Greece, the gods of Olympus were believed to have all of the characteristics of common people except one—mortality. When a common mortal died, it was forever.

When one of the gods was killed, it was only for a time. An artifact from 400 B.C. shows one of the gods giving a grand feast for all of his divine friends who had mourned his death in a game. Now the game was over.

As civilization emerged, the Greeks took for themselves the characteristics they ascribed to their gods, but only "citizens," few in number, could have these characteristics. The barbarians, the noncitizens of Greek culture, remained very mortal. Plato was a citizen, not a barbarian, and his philosophy of the soul, which has had so much influence on Western thought, reflected the notion that a human being, at least as a soul, has the potential of being as immortal as a god. Despite Plato's wisdom, his thought was not widely accepted for many generations after his death.

By the time of the Common Era many peoples in the Mediterranean region, including the ruling Romans, believed that the god of death was the most powerful of deities. Even some of the Semites believed death had ultimate power.

A small group of Hebrews were convinced that while death was very powerful, it was not supreme. When one of them, Jesus of Nazareth, who was believed by the Romans to be spreading sedition, was crucified at Calvary, the event was seen even by his followers as the final power of death. Later according to their accounts, even though Jesus was crucified, dead, and buried, on the third day he was raised up from the dead by God. This event revealed that even death is subject to the God of life. For those who saw the event as release from the power of death, life became new. It was a resurrection for them, too. They saw people's attempts to be perfect—to ascribe to themselves the characteristics of God—as the sin of pride which, rather than preserving life, cuts people off from the source of life.

When Christianity became politically acceptable throughout the Mediterranean region, the old Greek idea of human perfectibility and the ideal for striving for immortality still found many believers. They accommodated their beliefs to the new religion by teaching the injuction: "Be perfect, like Jesus," and by proclaiming that Jesus had become so perfect in nature, he had raised himself up from the dead, thereby indicating that all people can become immortal if we will but do, think, or feel the right things.

The struggle between the Greek and the Hebrew visions of human nature still exists, and many patients discover that their emotional conflicts are an embodiment of contradictory and competing claims for allegiance. Like the questions of the Puritans, the patient's question, "If it be the will of the Lord, am I willing to die for his glory?" was not only instructive, but self-revelatory. In that revelation, many patients feel relieved—and triumphant.

BUT WHAT ENDING FOR LIFE?

As relieved as some patients are in being released from their conflicts, some sense there is still the possibility of losing their victory. As in John Bunyan's *The Pilgrim's Progress*, hell is never closer than at heaven's door. Bunyan wrote his allegory about humanity's struggles with living. The pilgrim's road, he thought, is mined with traps, temptations, and terrors, any one of which could destroy the pilgrim's hopes for destiny. Even before the gates of heaven, there is a final test—a trap door that opens directly into hell.

You may think that Bunyan's vocabulary is antiquated. Perhaps you don't use the words *heaven* or *hell*. Many of the patients in our research group didn't either. Some of them disavowed any belief in "afterlife," "eternity," "heaven," or "hell." Nevertheless, they were still concerned about how life would end. They hoped that they would end life with a sense of purpose completed, a sense of destiny. Whatever the choice of vocabulary, basic to the concept of heaven is the meaning of life fulfilled or completed. Basic to the concept of hell is the sense that life is incomplete, finished, or alienated.

Some patients, particularly those who were in intensive care units or who had survived traumatic kinds of accidents, reported that before their conditions had stabilized, all they could think about was the horror of their life being cut off. "This just can't be happening to me," one girl kept saying to herself. "I'm too young!" She reported that she was shocked by the unexpected accident, but she was horrified by the memories of "all the terrible times of my life. My life seemed so meaningless. It was just hell!"

Other accident victims reported that even though they knew they were dying, they felt no fear or horror. In recorded testimony, some Swiss ski-accident survivors who thought they were dying reported that beautiful memories of their lives passed through their minds as they were falling. Their only anxiety was what they saw registered on the faces of their rescuers.[8]

Age seems to have some effect on the interpretation people have of dying. Some young or middle-aged patients expressed deep anger about their life being cut short. Many older patients not only thought death was appropriate but looked forward to the relief it would bring. In a study conducted for the National Institute of Mental Health, 55 percent of the old people in good health seemed to have resolved their struggles with death, 30 percent manifested denial, and 15 percent expressed alarm.

Mrs. P was one of those who had already resolved her struggle with dying. A 66-year-old former schoolteacher, she was born and reared in a "religious" family. She had married a man from a similar background and together they lived out what she called "a quest for value." Mrs. P was widowed at age 40. She finished the rearing of their two daughters who were now married with families of their own, and she retired from her career.

Mrs. P was confined to the hospital for the last three weeks of her life. Like many terminal patients, she had a sense of timing about the approach of her end. Friends were requested to visit, and without being either morbid or lengthy, she spoke to each in turn on what they had meant to her. She had written out instructions for her daughters about the disposition of her belongings and the kind of disposal she preferred for her body. When friends were uneasy in her presence or tried to play games about the reality of the situation, she very calmly, yet strongly, assured them: "We don't have to be afraid. Parting is difficult so let's cry together for a little while; then we can talk." That is what they would do. Several days before she died, she called together each daughter with her family and celebrated their reunion. Her business done, she asked an old and dear friend to be with her until the end. As she grew weaker, there was less and less conversation, but words were not necessary. She died in the manner for which she prepared—at peace.

It is doubtful that anyone could have broken Mrs. P's spirits. She was too disciplined and experienced in her faith. Those who have not had her experience, even though they may sense victory over their fears of dying, can be entrapped by the panic and alienation felt by those around them. Emma is an example.

Emma was elderly. She was also very bitter. She had been resuscitated following a cardiac arrest. "I remember going to sleep. It was so peaceful. Then there was this terrible intrusion, like an alarm clock going off in my ear. I've always hated alarm clocks; I would think

I was having a heart attack they startled me so. That was what it was like when the doctor brought me back, only more so, and I can remember thinking, 'Who is this intruder?' I shall never forgive him. Never!"

It was very hard for the physician to understand why Emma was not grateful to him for saving her life. In the conflict between them is revealed the difference between a life ending alienated and a life ending fulfilled. When we understand that the meaning a patient gives to life may be far more valuable than preservation of vital signs, we can serve the patient rather than our own fears. Emma had completed her life, only to be called back. "For what purpose?" she kept demanding. As in Bunyan's allegory, at the very gates of heaven Emma was pushed through a trap door of chaos into a state of alienated hell by an overly anxious physician.

Jack's life could have ended like Emma's, but it didn't. Jack was a young, husky, and handsome truck driver who was mangled in a highway accident and arrived conscious at the emergency room. Appearing to struggle for survival with every ounce of energy he could muster, his spirit inspired the emergency room staff to the limits of their talents. The sounds of the brisk orders, the rustle of the staff's rapid movements, the whining of the emergency equipment seemed to stimulate his adrenaline even more. Jack's injuries were too severe. The staff's frantic last efforts could have panicked him had it not been for the comforting words of the nun who made the emergency room her arena for ministry. Leaning close to his ear, she called him by name and said, "You're in good hands, Jack." Barely audible, his last words were, "Thank you for reminding me, Sister."

Life completed is life related, invested with love, and full of meaning. Whatever a patient's age, whatever a patient's crisis, love unsevered by dying is living in triumph.

Any patient can be thwarted in the attempt to complete a desired end, and many are. Sometimes patients are thwarted by lifelong patterns of uncertainly and avoidance; sometimes they are frustrated with a weak sense of identity. Sometimes, however, they are panicked by the behavior of overly anxious relatives and health care staff. Our task is to support our loved ones in their attempts to resolve their conflicts even when we ourselves feel helpless, in conflict, or hopeless. It may be that if we allow ourselves to be instructed by the dying, we ourselves will be relieved from that which binds us to death.

WHAT MEANING HAS TRIUMPH?

One of the hardest things for me to learn from critically and terminally ill patients was that my own feelings of anxiety blinded me from sharing their perceptions. Often the perceptions of the patients are in sharp contrast to the interpretations of the onlookers. Yet, when I became able to grant patients their own perceptions, I was able to discover how dying can mean triumph. To overcome fears that have tyrannized living, to conquer doubts that love can prevail, to discover who "I am," was a victory of great prize for almost all patients.

Something strange and beautiful often happens when a patient comes to the end of life. All fear, all horror seem to disappear. "I have often watched a look of happy wonder dawn in his eyes when he realized what was happening," writes a veteran nurse. "He seemed to come alive in a new form." I concur.

As patients no longer must live with pretense about their natures, when they give up plotting and calculating how to preserve their lives, when they no longer have to avoid dying because of their fears of death—then, ironically, the meaning of living takes on the characteristics of new life. Sometimes tranquilly, sometimes with a smile, other times with bursts of joy, patients express relief in the destruction of their last enemy. They are no longer subjects of death. What time there was to live—and for some it was only a moment—they can now love the gift of life that was given them. It is the time "when the perishable puts on the imperishable, and the mortal puts on immortality" (1 Cor. 15:54). For the time has come when they can confess: "Death is swallowed up in victory. O death, where is thy victory? O death, where is thy sting?" (1 Cor. 15:54-55).

Death dethroned! This is the meaning of dying in triumph. It is a lesson that has been shared from the deathbed for generations. It is shared now by those who, in many instances, are making their last gift, given for those of us who have yet to experience it. It won't be easy, it won't be without great struggle, but for those of us who mourn, to know that dying need not cut us off from the love that has made living worthwhile is the most comforting reassurance I can imagine.

Appendix

Some Models for Mourners

Grief is the normal reaction to death of a loved one, whether the death was sudden or anticipated. It is characterized by inner questioning, depressed moods, restlessness, loss of interest in the affairs of others, sleep disturbance, loss of appetite, or weight loss. If the hurts of the bereaved are to heal, normal reaction should also include ventilation of emotions, such as crying.

The common mistake of mourners is attempting to hide their grief, to try processing their feelings by themselves. Solitude is appropriate at times, but feelings of loss are easily transformed into loneliness, and loneliness is easily translated into feelings of alienation. The more lonely mourners become, the less likely they will find healthy release from sorrow.

If you are a mourner, several of the following models of assistance may help you handle your grief in a healthier manner.

ONE-TO-ONE COUNSELING

Sometimes we try to bottle up our emotions by maintaining the pretense that nothing has happened when we have lost someone very dear. The very fact that we are bereaved is evidence that something basic has happened and to maintain the pretense adds to the burden of our sorrow. It also adds to our health hazards.

Even for those mourners who express their grief openly, the presence of a sympathetic listener helps the process of adapting to loss. Clergy, social workers, psychiatric nurses, funeral directors, lawyers, trust officers, and even sympathetic laypersons can be effective in assisting mourners to make decisions, confirm and assess loss, regain perspective, establish new priorities for living, and discover new interests. The basic need is for someone who can listen sympathetically without being threatened by the mourner's ventilation of emotions or exaggeration of feelings. It is being able "to share my innermost feelings without having to worry about consequences," as one widow put it.

While one-to-one counseling is an effective model for initial processing of grief, it should not be used exclusively. The goal for individual counseling ought to be assisting the mourner to function more effectively in a social context. If individual counseling is sustained, it can deteriorate into unnecessary and untherapeutic dependencies.

HOSPICES

The hospice movement represents the greatest citizen-initiated change in health care delivery in North American history. From the founding of the first program in 1974, to the more than 2000 local programs in 1990, citizens are insisting that care for the terminally ill and their families be part of the spectrum of care in our society.

Hospice philosophy is an affirmation of life and a rejection of the presuppositions either that dying should be a taboo subject or that death is an unnatural event. Proponents of hospice philosophy affirm that while dying is an expected and normal process, many terminally ill patients and their families need support—physiologically, psychologically and spiritually—in order to live as fully and as comfortably as possible until death.

Different groups have articulated the hospice philosophy in various ways. Generally, however, all programs affirm the following principles:

- Dying is a normal part of living;
- Palliation is the treatment goal;
- Both patients and their closest companions—family and friends—constitute the unit of care;
- The spectrum of care should include support for survivors throughout their bereavement;
- An interdisciplinary team, including volunteers, is best able to provide the spectrum of necessary care.

For additional information write National Hospice Organization, 1901 N. Moore St., Suite 901, Arlington VA 22209.

MAKE TODAY COUNT

Founded by Orville Kelly, an Iowa newsman with cancer, "Make Today Count" (MTC) is an organization that helps cancer patients cope openly with their feelings and assists them in relating better to the mourning of their loved ones. The motto for the program is: "Don't think of the future. Just get the most out of each minute of each day."

The people who wrestle most effectively with reactions to cancer are cancer patients who know how to tap their own emotional resources and who are willing to share with others. The chapters of MTC are designed less for exchanges of agonies, however, than for matter-of-fact sharing about problem solving. MTC encourages cancer patients to communicate with one another, in group meetings if possible, or by telephone. For more information about the work of MTC, write: Make Today Count, Inc., 101½ S. Union St., Alexandria VA 22314.

SHARE

Founded in 1977 in Springfield, Ill., by parents who had lost a baby through miscarriage or stillbirth, this mutual-help group has expanded with chapters now in most states and several countries. The uniqueness of the original chapter is its providing support for parents out of the hospital context, which allows for immediate intervention, coordinated assistance from health care personnel, and follow-up assessment by SHARE parents. The group has succeeded in reforming many hospital protocols that unwittingly had added to parents' sorrow.

Mothers and fathers experiencing this loss need to learn how to seek as much, if not more, pampering, concern, affection, and attention to their needs as do parents whose baby has survived. SHARE provides a newsletter, extensive publications and audiovisual materials. International headquarters: SHARE, St. Elizabeth Hospital, 211 S. Third St., Belleville IL 62222. Other organizations for parents of newborn loss are: AMEND, 4324 Berrywick Terrace, St. Louis MO 63128; Resolve through Sharing, Gunderson Clinic, 1910 South Ave., La Crosse WI 54601. For parents who lose children of any age, The Compassionate Friends has chapters throughout North America. Headquarters address: P.O. Box 3696, Oakbrook IL 60522.

SUDDEN INFANT DEATH ALLIANCE

Local chapters for parents who have lost infants to Sudden Infant Death Syndrome have a twofold purpose: (1) to support research of SIDS, and (2) to assist families who may be suffering needless guilt based on uninformed notions about the disease.

SIDS strikes between two and three babies out of every 1000 births and accounts for 85 percent of unexpected infant deaths. It can neither be predicted nor prevented, even by a physician. The Old Testament referred to SIDS as "overlaying" (1 Kings 3:19). Folklore calls it "crib death" or "cot death" and usually attributes it to suffocation. Apparently because of a nearly instantaneous death, there is sometimes spasm, which leads the discovering parent to wrongly assume that the infant has been suffocated by bed clothes, has choked on vomit, or has been maltreated.

Parents suffer not only from the shock of their infant's unexpected death but from the suspicions of relatives, police personnel, coroners, and others, who jump to the conclusion that malicious neglect is self-evident. Young couples have been jailed by vindictive officials who fail to distinguish between victims of SIDS and perpetrators of child abuse, thus making the suffering of the parents all the more acute.

Local SIDS chapters attempt to educate public officials about the nature of the disease, intervene on behalf of stricken parents as quickly as possible, and refer parents to competent counselors. Most SIDS chapters are not designed to give professional counseling services.

As a model for mourners, these organizations fill the needs of on-the-spot and prompt intervention that both shields the mourners while they are in the depths of shock and assists them in getting competent assistance.

Studies at the University of Washington show that parents of SIDS victims tend to be far more depressed than parents of children who die of better-known diseases and whose deaths were anticipated. The same studies also demonstrate the need for giving assistance to siblings who may feel guilty because of normal feelings of ambivalence about loss of their younger rival.

For further information, write your state health department, or SIDS Alliance, 330 N. Charles St., Baltimore MD 21201.

WIDOW-TO-WIDOW AND WIDOWER PROGRAMS

If one-to-one counseling is appropriate for helping individual mourners in the initial period of grief or when they are having difficulty resolving conflicts of loss, programs such as widow-to-widow and widower groups are appropriate for helping mourners become reoriented to a social context.

A mourner may protest, "But I don't want anyone else to know how much I hurt," or "I don't need to hear anyone else's problems; I have enough of my own." In doing so this mourner reveals not the need for solitude but the fear of rejection because of grieving. A number of sorrowing relatives and friends report that after the death of their loved one, they knew how important it was to ventilate emotions and work through feelings of conflict, but when they tried to do so, it embarrassed the people around them. "Now I know what Fred went through when he tried to talk to us about dying," one widow confessed. Groups of people coming together at times of need can provide a social context for healing that may not otherwise be available to the mourner. In a group, mourners can look at common problems, get experienced assistance in assessing feelings of loss, find moral support in working out solutions to problems, and as important as any of the above, share in turn with others who have been hurt by loss of a loved one.

Widowers in particular may need assistance reorienting themselves to social contexts. A study by the National Center for Health Statistics indicates that the death rate for America's 2 million widowers is double that of married men in comparable age categories above the age of 45. For white widowers between the ages of 20 and 34, the death rate is the highest for any segment of the male population. Major causes of death for them are vascular diseases, lung and stomach cancers, cirrhosis of the liver, and arteriosclerotic heart disease, indicating direct and indirect connections between incomplete or inadequate mourning and physical and mental breakdown.

Some churches, associations of funeral directors, and mental health associations have organized groups for mourners. Call your pastor, local hospital pastoral care department, or social service office to find the nearest group available for you. For assistance with organizing a group, write: American Association of Retired Persons, Widowed Persons Service, 1909 "K" St. N.W., Washington D.C. 20049; or THEOS (They Help Each Other Spiritually), 717 Liberty Ave., Clark Bldg. #1301, Pittsburgh PA 15222.

PARENTS WITHOUT PARTNERS

For some mourners, feelings of grief must compete with the responsibilities of raising dependent children. Parents Without Partners, Inc., with chapters across the country, provides crisis intervention centers, research, and public education programs on the problems for single parents. It also provides referral services for various agencies that have special competencies for working with children and educational and social programs for parents and their children. The goals of the organization focus on endeavors to bring children to healthy maturity, and to overcome the problems of being an isolated parent in society. The mailing address for the international headquarters is P.O. Box 700, Clinton MD 20795.

OTHER ORGANIZATIONS THAT CAN BE OF ASSISTANCE

American Association of Suicidology
2459 S. Ash St.
Denver, CO 80222

Association for Death Education and
    Counseling
533 Stagg Lane
Santa Cruz, CA 95062

National AIDS Information Clearinghouse
P.O. Box 6003
Rockville, MD 20850

National Funeral Directors Association
11121 W. Oklahoma Ave.
Milwaukee, WI 53227

Parents of Murdered Children
100 E. Eighth St., B-41
Cincinnati, OH 45202

Notes

1. Sr. Mary Catherine O'Conner. *The Art of Dying Well* (New York: Columbia University Press, 1942), p. 4.
2. Erna Furman, "Children's Patterns in Mourning the Death of a Loved One," in Wass and Corr, eds., *Childhood and Death* (New York: Hemisphere Publishing Corp., 1984), pp. 185-203.
3. From the research of Anna Freud and H. Hartmann, cited by Humberto Nagera. See his "Children's Reactions to the Death of Important Objects," *Psychoanalytic Study of the Child*, Vol. 25 (1970), pp. 360-400.
4. David Elkind. *All Grown Up & No Place to Go: Teenagers in Crisis* (Reading, MA: Addison-Wesley Publishing Co., 1984).
5. John Bowlby and C. Murray Parkes, "Separation and Loss Within the Family," in E. James Anthony and Cyrille Koupernik, *The Child in His Family* (New York: John Wiley & Sons, 1970), pp. 197-98.
6. Other metaphors have been used by my former colleagues. Elisabeth Kübler-Ross used the metaphor, "stage," to describe a patient's characteristic behavior based on early findings of the Chicago "Program on Death and Dying." See her book, *On Death and Dying* (New York: Macmillan Company, 1969). The late Carl Nighswonger used the metaphor, "drama." See his article, "Ministry to the Dying as a Learning Encounter," *Journal of Thanatology*, Vol. 1, No. 2 (March/April 1971).

7. M. Holmes Hartshorne, "The Grace of Suffering," a sermon preached in the Colgate University Chapel, May 3, 1964.
8. Russell Noyes Jr., "The Experience of Dying," *Psychiatry*, Vol. 35 (May 1972).

Selected Bibliography

Aries, Philippe. *The Hour of Our Death.* New York: Alfred A. Knopf, 1981.

The Book of Services. Nashville: The United Methodist Publishing House, 1985.

Bowlby, John. *Attachment and Loss,* vol. III. New York: Basic Books, 1980.

Davidson, Glen W. *Hospice: Development and Administration,* 2nd ed. Washington, D.C.: Hemisphere Publishing Corporation, 1985.

Davidson, Glen W. *Understanding Mourning.* Minneapolis: Augsburg, 1984.

Death Studies: Education, Counseling, Care, Law, Ethics. A scholarly journal published bimonthly by Hemisphere Publishing Corporation, Washington, D.C.

DeSpelder, Lynne Ann and Albert Lee Strickland. *The Last Dance: Encountering Death and Dying.* Palo Alto, CA: Mayfield, 1983.

Elkind, David. *All Grown Up & No Place To Go: Teenagers In Crisis.* Reading, MA: AddisonWesley Publishing Company, 1984.

Lamb, Sr. Jane Marie, ed. *Bittersweet . . . Hello Goodbye: A Resource in Planning Farewell Rituals When a Baby Dies.* Springfield, IL: Prairie Lark Press, Box 699, 1988.

Lonetto, Richard. *Children's Conceptions of Death.* Vol. 3, The Springer Series on Death and Suicide. New York: Springer Publishing Company, 1980.

Lutheran Book of Worship. Minneapolis: Augsburg Fortress, 1978.

McGill, Arthur C. *Suffering: A Test of Theological Method.* Philadelphia: Westminster, 1982.

Numbers, Ronald L. and Darrel W. Amundsen, eds. *Caring and Curing: Health and Medicine in the Western Religious Traditions.* New York: Macmillan Publishing Company, 1986.

Raphael, Beverley. *The Anatomy of Bereavement.* New York: Basic Books, 1983.

Schuchardt, Erika. *Why Is This Happening to Me?* Minneapolis: Augsburg, 1989.

Stein, Sara Bonnett. *About Dying: An Open Family Book for Parents and Children Together.* Photography by Dick Frank. New York: Walker and Company, 1974.

Stillion, Judith and Hannelore Wass. *Death: Current Perspectives.* Palo Alto, CA: Mayfield, 1984.

Wass, Hannelore and Charles Corr. *Childhood and Death.* Washington, D.C.: Hemisphere Publishing Corp., 1984.

Wass, Hannelore and Charles Corr. *Helping Children Cope With Death: Guidelines and Resources.* Washington, D.C.: Hemisphere Publishing Corporation, 1982.

Westberg, Granger. *Good Grief.* Minneapolis: Fortress Press, 1971.